CAPE*CORAL BURROWING OWLS DON'T HOOT

BEVERLY AHLERING SALTONSTALL

Copyright 2023 by Beverly Ahlering Saltonstall

ISBN: 979-8863131634

Imprint: Independently published

For information about this title, contact the author

Contact@capecoralowls.com

Printed in the United States

Contents

Cape Coral Burrowing Owls

Photo by Beverly Ahlering Saltonstall

All the photos in this book, except where noted, were taken with a Nikon SX50 with an extended lens or a D950 with a 2000 mm lens, allowing me to take incredibly close photographs from a very safe distance away, including my living room.

We send thanks to all the animal life in the world. They have many things to teach us people. We are glad they are still here, and we hope it will always be so.

Excerpt from the Thanksgiving Address, Mohawk version

PREFACE

The two men waited for a moonless night, parked their car down the street, and inched slowly towards the empty lot ahead, scanning the area to be sure no one was watching them. Quietly, they walked over to a small mound of dirt and began shoveling, quickly trying to fill in the small hole they found. Suddenly, seemingly out of nowhere, a tiny bird came screeching over their heads, making every attempt to chase the two men away.

Back in the earlier days of Cape Coral, some people thought you could not build on a property where a Burrowing Owl was living. They would go out in the middle of the night to cover up the burrows the owls had dug, then they could tell the city there were no owls on the property when they wanted to build a home or business. Thanks go out for the dedication of Sue Scott, Carol Keifer, and Jackie O'Connell, who got the ball rolling to protect the Burrowing Owls of Cape Coral. Hopefully, this practice will occur with less frequency. This book is dedicated to those ladies, Cape Coral Friends of Wildlife, and its members who tirelessly work to help the Burrowing Owls and all wildlife here in Cape Coral.

I would be amiss if I didn't thank Barbara Brown and Fran Yorkston for helping me with this book and Carl Veaux, Cheryl Anderson, and Bernadette McNee for all their hard work.

This book is especially dedicated to Pascha Donaldson, who has done so much to get the City Council to pass and enforce legislation to help the city's owls and other wildlife. I am sure I have missed some people, but others have made this a better place for all the wildlife of Cape Coral, which has made this a better place for the residents and visitors to Cape Coral.

To set the record straight, I am not a biologist or a scientist. I am a retired Registered Nurse, and from the first time I saw a Burrowing Owl's beautiful eyes, I was hooked and have been working with them ever since. They dragged me out of my comfort zone into doing things I would never have imagined. Had you asked me ten years ago if I would be a guest speaker at an Audubon Society meeting or be a tour guide, I would have flat-out told you that you were crazy. If you had asked me if it was OK that NatGeoWild could interview me and ultimately appear on one of their TV shows, I would have asked you what you were smoking. Today, I love talking to anyone who will listen to me about owls. I speak to school children through college students and take ornithologists, brain surgeons, and people from all over the world out to see these owls. I love sharing my love for these owls with people and being a part of the enjoyment; they get from seeing them for the first time.

I wanted to see the cute and quirky Burrowing Owls of Cape Coral, Florida, remembered in a book, so I wrote it! This book is everything I know about Burrowing Owls. Neurology is too deep a subject to include, but I have included personal stories you may enjoy.

Figure 2 Juvenile Burrowing Owl

CHAPTER 1   The Early Days

To understand how Cape Coral became the Burrowing Owl "epicenter," one needs to know a bit about Florida's history and the surrounding area. The earth is estimated to be about four and a half billion years old, and Florida is nearly 530 million years old. Florida was originally part of the Gondwana supercontinent. As plate tectonics moved Gondwana westward, it collided with another continent, Laurasia, and formed the supercontinent of Pangea. The colliding of these continents sandwiched Florida between the Americas and Africa. Hence, Florida shares the same sandy soil structure as Senegal, Africa, unlike the rock formations found in North America.

Between 190 and 66 million years ago, the Florida plateau was underwater several times, explaining why the soil is mainly calcium carbonate or better known as limestone. Still today, two-thirds of the plateau that makes up Florida lies underwater. A huge aquifer lies underground, and the limestone's gradual dissolving has helped create widespread sinkholes across the State.

Fast forward to about 12-14,000 years ago, and you have the first archeological evidence of humans in Florida. With so much water in Florida, the early Native American tribes in Southwest Florida relied on hunting, fishing, and gathering as their mainstay diet. With the Europeans' arrival in the 1500s, disease, wars, and slavery eradicated many tribes, and today, only two Federally recognized tribes remain in Florida, the Miccosukee and Seminole Indians, both living on reservations.

Fast forward again to the 1900s in Southwest Florida. The native Calusa Indians have been gone since the 1700s, and few people lived in the area that was to become Cape Coral. The area's inhabitants were primarily fishermen, settlers, farmers, and some citrus growers. With the lack of air-conditioning, high humidity, heat, and mosquitoes in Southwest Florida, and most of Florida, it was not a great place to live.

With the arrival of Thomas Edison, Henry Ford, and Harvey Firestone to Fort Myers in the late 1800s, things began to boom. According to Florida Backroads Travel, "Southwest Florida heritage and history have been affected simply by the fact that these three famous men chose to winter here. It brought huge national publicity to the region."

"The history of Southwest Florida covers many backgrounds. You will find old Florida country towns with a cattle heritage and some affluent towns. In the 1920s, during Prohibition, Naples was reported to have 26 millionaires and 22 rum runners. Fast boats made runs from Cuba and the Bahamas to Naples for pleasure trips and nefarious reasons. From these humble beginnings, Southwest Florida has grown to a population of 1.3 million people."

In the 1950s, when I was a kid, I remember a joke going around where people would say in a low tone of voice, "Hey buddy, you want to buy land in Florida?" People would laugh, saying they were selling swampland! The "swampland" (which was actually wetlands) they were selling eventually became the thriving community of Cape Coral. The Rosen brothers, investors from Baltimore, flew down to southwest Florida to buy land to build the largest master-planned community in the United States. What they found was a peninsula off the peninsula of Florida itself. Lying west of Fort Myers, on the western side of the Caloosahatchee River, was a spit of land surrounded on three sides by water and nicely protected from the Gulf of Mexico by the barrier islands of Estero, Sanibel, Captiva, North Captiva, and Cayo Costa. To the east and south was the Caloosahatchee River, a recreational and commercial waterway. The Caloosahatchee River is a part of the Intracoastal Waterway (ICW). This water route runs from New Jersey down the east coast of the United States through Florida, connecting with the Caloosahatchee River and continuing to Brownsville, Texas. Boaters using this waterway can travel from New Jersey to Texas without going out in open water. Added to this beautiful location was the fact that the fishing here was world-renowned, as people from all over came to nearby Boca Grande, the "Tarpon Fishing Capital of the World."

The Rosen Brothers thought this would be a wonderful place to build their "Water Wonderland" and purchased the 100+ square mile parcel of land for about $678,000, the price of a lovely home in Cape Coral today.

Two reads must be on your list if you are interested in Cape Coral's history. First is Cape Coral's history, Lies that Came True, by Eileen Bernard, and a story from Politico Magazine, with an incredibly long title, The Boomtown That Shouldn't Exist, Cape Coral, Florida, was built on total lies. One big storm could wipe it off the map. Oh, and it's also one of the fastest-growing cities in the United States. The book, Lies that Came True can be found at the local libraries, and The Boomtown that Shouldn't Exist article can be found by doing a Google search on the Internet.

This is my five-plus million-year history of the area in a nutshell.

Cape Coral's Recent History

Prior to the 1950s, Cape Coral's "downtown" area was lowlands and prime habitat for many water birds, such as herons, egrets, and roseate spoonbills. This area would flood with storms; since it is at sea level, the water naturally rose and fell with tidal changes. The northern portion of the peninsula was higher in elevation and consisted mainly of Pine Flatwoods, which is the type of habitat that covers nearly 50% of Florida's land. This wooded area was a habitat for bobcats, squirrels, box turtles, deer, possums, hawks, woodpeckers, gopher tortoises, bald eagles, black bears, and the endangered Florida panther.

According to the book The Other Side of the River: Historical Cape Coral by B Zeiss, homesteaders lived in the area and used the land for agricultural purposes and cattle ranching. Reportedly, orange groves were in the area, and people came from Fort Myers to hunt quail. That is about all that was happening in the area at the time in those early days.

Figure 3 As far as the eyes can see

Once the Rosen brothers began building the community, they brought in the most extensive collection of earthmoving equipment that had ever been seen in Florida. The wetlands were filled in; the Flatwoods were cleared, and they dug 400 miles of canals. The properties were divided into land parcels measuring 40' x 125' feet, and at least two of these parcels were needed to build a home. A massive selling campaign was launched, and the Rosen brothers and their employees went worldwide selling these properties. What was once miles and miles of lush Florida habitat was now miles and miles of empty land. Figure 3 shows the vast expanses of empty land which still exist today, as seen in this recent photo.

Cape Coral Parkway, the main road in the area, became an airstrip, and people from all over were flown in to show them available properties. According to a resident who was a pilot then, flights ran from 10:00 a.m. until 3:00 p.m., because they did not want the visitors to know how bad the mosquitos were outside those hours. Many people purchased building lots sight unseen, and others, even if they later visited the area, had no idea where the lots they bought were located. History tells us that interesting sales techniques were used to persuade people to buy properties.

Construction was not without its drawbacks, one of which was the massive loss of habitat for the wildlife that lived here. As construction progressed, the wetlands and the woodlands were destroyed, and the large mangrove stands surrounding the peninsula were also torn down. The mangrove stands that offered protection from the fierce storms that often battered the area provided wildlife habitat, shelter for newly spawned fish, and were critical for maintaining good water quality, was cleared for homesites. While massive destruction of wildlife habitat led to the loss of much of wildlife that lived here, fortunately, some wildlife survived.

We still have a thriving population of Gopher Tortoises, Bald Eagles, Ibis, and Raccoons. In one section of town, until recently, we had a small population of the Florida Scrub-jay, a threatened species that is the only endemic bird in Florida. (Endemic means you can only see this bird in Florida and nowhere else in the

FIGURE 4 FLORIDA SCRUB-JAY

world.) Biologists felt the habitat was not suitable for the Scrub-jays and they would not survive long term there.

This area is slated to become a park and the development of the park accelerated the demise of the birds and the birds are no longer found at the site.

In 1970, Cape Coral was incorporated and officially became a city. It is the second-largest city, land-wise, in the State of Florida, with over 100 square miles of land. The city's projected build-out was to be 400,000 people based on having single-family homes, but money talks, and now high-rise buildings are allowed, so the projected population was increased to 450,000 people. As of 2022, there were nearly 200,000 residents living in Cape Coral.

The Burrowing Owls

Late in the 1800s, an article appeared in Sportsman Magazine reporting that the first Burrowing Owl was found near Sarasota, Florida. Cindy Bear, a local biologist who has researched the Cape Coral owls in the past, told me there were Burrowing Owls in the county (Lee County) as far back as the 1900s, but it is unknown when Burrowing Owls arrived in Cape Coral. The earliest record of a Burrowing Owl in Cape Coral that I can find is in 1968 during the Christmas Bird Count conducted by the Caloosa Bird Club. In speaking to a resident who lived in Cape Coral in the early 1970s, there were lots of Burrowing Owls living in Cape Coral then. This would suggest that there was a significant population of Burrowing Owls living in the Cape before the late 1960s, possibly on the cattle ranches that were in the area, but in general, the habitat was not what Burrowing Owls would find suitable. What is known is that with the miles and miles of canals, living on the water was a big draw for many people. With the reasonable price of homes here, the town was thriving, but with all the miles and miles of soft sandy soil and empty lots, the owls also loved Cape Coral. This town was a win-win situation for both humans and the Burrowing Owls.

The Years 2000-2001

Figure 5 Adult Burrowing Owl

As fast as the people moved in, the Burrowing Owl population grew as well. Things were moving along quite well in Cape Coral, and around the year 2001, a couple of things important to this story happened. First off, the city had a big party to celebrate its 100,000th resident. That party was a lot of fun and was one of the first things I attended as a new resident. Then the first owl vs. human issue occurred. As I mentioned before, the sales team for this planned community went worldwide selling properties, and many people from overseas own properties in Cape Coral. These property owners could not make regular trips to Cape Coral to take care of the vegetation on their properties, and overgrown vegetation had become a problem. To solve the problem, the city purchased several lot mowers to cut the vegetation and sent the lot owners a bill for the service. That worked well, except for the properties where the owls lived. Burrowing Owls blend in with the sandy soil we have here in Florida, so they are difficult to spot. Even if the lot mower saw the owls, the burrows could be 10 feet long, so the lot mowers could still be running over the nest chamber where the chicks and the female owls live. These huge machines were no match for these tiny little birds.

FIGURE 6 LOT MOWER

Florida Wildlife Conservation Commission (FWCC) was concerned about this problem and instructed the city to install stakes around the burrows to alert the lot mowers that a burrow was present on the lot. At that time, the City Council and most city officials were in what I call a "build mentality." They were focused on building Cape Coral out to its full capacity, and the Burrowing Owls were a bit of a nuisance to them. There was probably only one person employed in the city then that cared about the owls, Sue Scott: the Planning Technician. The city gave her a hammer, stakes, and the job of marking all the burrows in town. No one knew how many burrows there were then, but when Cape Coral did a survey about eight years later, 2700 burrows were counted, so there must have been quite a few when Sue started the staking project. Sue started putting out four wooden stakes and a T-perch at every burrow she could find. It was a monumental job, and Sue quickly realized she needed help.

During this time, another issue emerged. Carol Kiefer, a resident of the Cape, had a Burrowing Owl living on the empty lot across the street from her home. When the lot mower came, the poor little owl was frightened and flew off the lot, only to return when the lot mower left. Carol spoke to her friend Jackie O'Connell about the poor little owl, and they decided they should go to the city about the problem. Off they went and were directed to Sue Scott to discuss their concern. After some back and forth with the city, Carol was granted permission to stake the burrow on that lot. One thing led to another, and the three ladies got permission to recruit volunteers to help with staking the burrows on a city-wide level.

FIGURE 7 ADULT BURROWING OWL ON A T-PERCH

The third thing that happened during this momentous time was that I moved to Florida. Not to be funny, but I am an early bird. The crack of dawn is my time to shine. When I first moved to Cape Coral from New Jersey, I would drive around in the early morning, checking out my new hometown. It was not long before I noticed something weird about Cape Coral. I began seeing wooden crosses on many of the empty lots and occasionally on people's front lawns. Were these pet cemeteries? Were Cape Coral residents' terrible drivers? What in the world were all these crosses all over the city?

While riding down one of the residential streets, I came to an empty lot and saw a tiny little bird with the most enchanting yellow eyes standing on top of one of those wooden crosses. There was a T-perch and a sign saying that it was a protected species site and warned people to stay away.

I was still confused by what I was seeing, and more so when the bird seemed unafraid of my parked car and my wide-open mouth as I sat in my car, gawking at the bird. The little bird stood there quietly, its head turning side-to-side and occasionally looking up at the sky. It seemed to be guarding something, but I had no clue what was going on. I watched it for a while and then slowly pulled

16

away. On my way home, I passed the same lot, and the little bird was still standing there in the same position, just watching and looking.

As a new homeowner, I was busy around the house and just filed this incident in the back of my brain for future exploration. As karma would have it, I noticed an article in the local newspaper a few days later. The City of Cape Coral was looking for volunteers to help with their Burrowing Owls, and a recruitment meeting was to take place a few days later. I had no idea what a Burrowing Owl was, but a quick scan of Stokes Bird Guide showed me that the bird I had seen standing on that cross was a Burrowing Owl. Since its range did not extend into the northeast portion of the United States, that explained why I had never seen one before.

Throughout my life, I have been active in many things. As a youngster, I played in a marching band, and I was the second-best jack player in our township; I was in Girl Scouts and a local hospital volunteer. As an adult, I have been involved in several service organizations, boating organizations, and many outdoor activities. On my retirement bucket list was an item to become more active in birding, so the chance to help a local bird was right up my alley.

About a dozen of us attended that meeting which was held at a local park. We sat around a picnic table and were told about the little Burrowing Owls. Unlike other wildlife, the Burrowing Owl can adapt to disturbed habitats, so it was ideal for these owls when Cape Coral developed into a prairie-like habitat. They like wide-open spaces to watch the skies for predators such as hawks, and they want soft sand where they can dig their burrows. Because of these ideal conditions, Cape Coral has the largest population of the Florida subspecies of the Burrowing Owl in the State of Florida, and Florida has the largest population of this subspecies. Since this subspecies is only found in Florida, southern Georgia, Alabama, and the Caribbean, Cape Coral technically has the world's largest population of the Florida Burrowing Owl (Athene cunicularia floridana).

FIGURE 8 WRECKED PERSONAL EQUIPMENT

We found out that the lot mowers could not always see the owls or their burrows, and since the burrows could extend as much as 10 feet in any direction from the burrow opening, it was easy to run over the burrow and trap the owls inside. Florida Fish and Wildlife wanted the burrows marked off, so we were the first volunteers to start the staking project. We took a training class on how not to collapse a burrow as we walked around it, how to scan the area so as not to scare the owls into the path of a car or a hawk, and how to place four stakes around the burrow as recommended by FWCC. We learned that some of the Western sub-species of the Burrowing Owls (Athene cunicularia hypugia) that live in Canada migrates to Mexico.

As a result, all Burrowing Owls fall under the Federal Migratory Bird Act passed in 1918, that implemented a treaty between Canada and the United States. This treaty protects many birds that migrate between the two countries, and even though the Florida Burrowing Owls do not migrate and are protected by this law. This means the bird, its eggs, its feathers, its chicks, and its burrow are protected by federal law.

What did this mean for Cape Coral? Once the Burrowing Owl nests were staked off, the lot mowers cut the vegetation around the outside of the stakes. Over time, the grass inside was getting overgrown, and the owls would abandon the burrow because they could not find the entrance, or predators could hide in the tall grass. Since the burrows are protected by federal law, even if the burrow was abandoned, you cannot just close a burrow; it requires a permit. As it would not be good to have all these abandoned burrows all over the city, we were further trained on how to trim the grass inside the stakes.

Our group started using our personal weed eaters and lawn equipment to cut the grass. After wearing out a lot of our equipment, as shown in Figure 8, the group met and decided that we should try to raise some money to purchase professional equipment. We held an organizational meeting, and the first order of business was to give our group a name, so we became Cape Coral Friends of Wildlife. The second order of business was to figure out how to raise money, and someone suggested that we have a festival. Everyone thought it was a great idea, but on the negative side, none of us had ever run a festival. Fortunately, the City Park and Recreation Department was a tremendous help and let us use Rotary Park, one of our local parks. We held the festival on a wing and a prayer, and to our amazement, it was an enormous success with over 2000 people attending. In 2021, we held our 19th Annual Festival as our first virtual festival because of the Covid-19 epidemic, but CCFW still raised over $9000 at that virtual festival.

So that is how it all started. Today, Cape Coral Friends of Wildlife is an organization of over 500 members and has made great strides in saving the Burrowing Owls, the Gopher Tortoise, butterflies, Purple Martins, Manatees, and other wildlife in Cape Coral.

Now let me tell you everything I know about Burrowing Owls.

FIGURE 9 WHERE IS CAPE CORAL?

CHAPTER 2 Fossils

Owls have been around for a long time, but owl fossils are hard to find. Dinosaur bones are massive and can survive millions of years, but owl bones are fragile and do not preserve well. With that said, "Ogygoptynx, the oldest owl fossil on record, was found in what is now Colorado and dates to about 61 million years ago, about four million years after the dinosaurs went extinct about 65 million years ago."

Three complete skeletons of what are believed to be the largest owls ever recorded were discovered in Cuba. The Cuban giant owl or giant cursorial owl (Ornimegalonyx) is an extinct genus of the Giant Owl that lived 10,000 years ago and measured "1.1 meters (3 ft 7 in) in height and weighed 9 kilograms (20 lb.). Because of its bulky size, it may have been flightless. The owl alive today that is its closest relative is the dainty Burrowing Owl."

"Fossils of Burrowing Owls (Speotyto megalopera), which were larger and more robust than the present species, have been found dating back 5.3 to 2.6 million years ago in Idaho deposits and Kansas.

The most current ice age began some 2.4 million years ago and lasted until about 11,500 years ago. Fossil remains that date back to the ice age of an extinct bird (A. c providentiae) was found in the Bahamas and may also be related to the current Florida Burrowing Owl (Athene cunicularia floridana). Fossils of a similar owl have been found throughout the Caribbean, on Barbuda, the Cayman Islands, Jamaica, Mona Island, and Puerto Rico. Because of environmental and sea-level changes, these birds became extinct at the end of the ice age. The first fossil of a presumed ancestor of the Burrowing Owl (Speotyto (Athene) megalopa), which dates to 2.6 million years ago, was found in Kansas, U. S. A.

CHAPTER 3 Range

Range of *A. cunicularia*
  Summer breeding range
  Winter non-breeding range
  Resident breeding range

Wikipedia , Burrowing Owl

FIGURE 10 BURROWING OWL RANGE

At one time in the not-so-distant past, Burrowing Owls were a frequent sight in the United States. Historically, colonies were sometimes large; Bent (1938) describes a Florida colony seen in the 1880s that was 3 miles (4.8 km) long and contained "several hundred" pairs of owls. Today, the western subspecies' range extends from areas west of the Mississippi River in the U.S. and from Canada to Tierra del Fuego on the west side of North and South America. The Florida subspecies are found in Florida, Georgia, Alabama, surrounding states, and the Caribbean. (above)

Development, agriculture, pesticides, and the destruction of prairie dog burrows for the Western species have resulted in a steep decline in these birds' numbers. Imperial Valley, home to nearly one-third of California's Burrowing Owl population, suffered a population decline of 27% IN ONE YEAR. And the owl population in Canada is down to 1000 nesting pairs. The Burrowing Owl's western subspecies is endangered in Canada, Iowa, and Minnesota and a species of special concern in California, Idaho, Kansas, Montana, Nebraska, Oklahoma, Oregon, South Dakota, Utah, and Washington. In 2018, FWCC changed the Florida subspecies of the Burrowing Owl from a species of special concern to a threatened status.

It is unknown how many Burrowing Owls there are in Florida, as estimates run from 3000 to 10,000, and Cape Coral has no accurate data to determine how many Burrowing Owls there are in the city. In 1987 and 2002, Florida Fish and Wildlife Conservation Commission conducted a Burrowing Owl study. Over five years, they counted and banded all the Burrowing Owls they could find in 13 square miles of the city. (The entire City of Cape Coral covers 100 square miles). From the data FWCC collected, they estimated 1000 nesting pairs of owls were in Cape Coral. (More than all of Canada)

In 2018, 125 volunteers made an unscientific count of the Burrowing Owls in Cape Coral. Several striking problems with the count were identified. First, volunteers needed more training to learn what the owls looked like and where to find the burrows. Second, owls are often just inside the burrow, making them difficult to see. Walking up to a burrow is strongly discouraged and illegal, as the burrows can collapse if stepped on. Finally, navigating the streets of Cape Coral is confusing at best. Almost every street is a dead-end because of the extensive canal system, and it is easy to lose track of which streets were driven. As of the writing of this book, the results of that study have not been completed, but preliminary estimates put the count at between 2500 and 3500 owls.

Several years after the original FWCC study, GPS trackers were placed on fifty Burrowing Owls. The location where the owls were released is unknown, so I will use an arbitrary site (the intersection of Santa Barbara Boulevard and Veterans Parkway) as an estimated distance of how far the owls traveled. Forty-five of the owls remained within three blocks of where they were released. One owl was tracked to Lakes Park (6.5 miles) in Fort Myers. A second owl was tracked to Lehigh Acres (21 miles), a third owl traveled to Northern Cape Coral (5 miles), and a fourth owl traveled to Marco Island (46 miles), where the second largest population of Burrowing Owls in Florida is located. The location of one owl was unknown.

I am often asked if owls can fly. This small GPS experiment showed that they can and do fly. In recent years, several sightings of wayward owls have been reported. Two years in a row, a Burrowing Owl was found as far north as Chicago, and one was spotted on a jetty in eastern North Carolina. One Burrowing Owl was found on a cruise ship's miniature golf course, where it thought it might make its home. It was removed before the ship left for the Caribbean, and recently one made it from Miami (FL) to Mexico on a cruise ship.

The range map below has been published by Florida Fish and Wildlife Conservation Commission (FWCC) and depicts the range of the Burrowing Owl in Florida. I would suspect that this shows where Burrowing Owls have been sighted in Florida, showing that they are found all over Florida except for the far north section. Elgin Air Force Base is the only place they are reported to be found in the Florida Panhandle. eBird, an online birding app, reports sightings of Burrowing Owls over the Florida border into lower Georgia and Alabama.

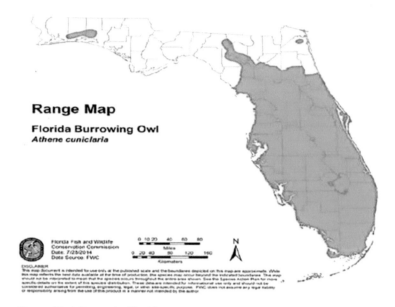

Figure 10-A Range in Florida

CHAPTER 4 Facts About the Burrowing Owls

Figure 11 Adult Burrowing Owl on left and on right is a juvenile Burrowing Owl

People are amazed to see a Burrowing Owl for the first time and are surprised at its small size. Below is a brief description of a Burrowing Owl.

On average, they are 7-9 inches tall.

They have short tails.

They have a long wingspan of 22-24 inches, which helps them fly in near silence. They have lighter buff-colored chests with more streaking.

They have white chins.

They have long featherless legs and are often seen standing on one leg.

Most have lemon-yellow eyes, but eye color varies in the Florida sub-species.

They have rounded heads with no tufts.

The juvenile looks like an adult, except it lacks the adult's chest barring.

They are seen standing on a perch in broad daylight during the day.

Juveniles make a sound like a rattlesnake to keep predators away from the burrow.

They are the only owl in the world that lives underground.

They can turn their heads 270° but not 360°.

CAPE CORAL BURROWING OWLS DON'T HOOT

There is usually no difference in size between males and females.

Females lay between 4 and 8 eggs, and incubation lasts 28 days. They live for up to 8 years in the wild

They have deep brown backs with spotting.

CHAPTER 5 Feathers

Fossil Feathers

What do Tyrannosaurus Rex and the Burrowing Owl have in common? In the 1860s, the hunt for the Burrowing Owls ancestor began with the discovery of a fossil of what was believed to be the first known bird, Archaeopteryx. Archaeopteryx, a 150-million-year-old fossil, was the first fossil with wings that showed there might be an evolutionary link between birds and dinosaurs. But paleontologists couldn't decide whether this winged animal could fly. With new scientific equipment available, scientists have been dusting off old fossils lying around in museums and looking at them with a fresh eye. Coupled with discoveries from China, South America, and other countries, the latest theory about the evolution of birds is that they may have evolved from a group of dinosaurs called theropods. So, it is hard to believe, but the dainty little Burrowing Owls (and all birds) are descended from a group of two-legged dinosaurs, the theropods. T-Rex and the velociraptors belong to the same family, so current thinking is that birds are the only dinosaurs that survived, and they survived because they had beaks and ate seeds. (Velociraptors are the dinosaurs made famous in the movie Jurassic Park). More amazing is the fact that our tiny Burrowing Owls belong to the same family at T-Rex.

In 2019, Cape Coral Friends of Wildlife was fortunate enough to have David Johnson, the Global Owl Project director, attend the Annual Burrowing Owl Festival and present a Burrowing Owl lecture. He showed several owl fossils slides with feathers estimated to be 58 million years old. He said that little is known about when the owls appeared, but finding those owl fossils confirms that owls have been around for at least 58 million years, and they were around when the meteor that caused the extinction of dinosaurs struck the earth. So, there is a lot of agreement that owls have been around for a long time.

Feathers

FIGURE 12 BURROWING OWL FEATHERS

Feathers distinguish birds from all other vertebrates, as no other vertebrates currently have structures resembling feathers. As can be expected, these feathers are essential and perform many distinct functions. The first and foremost function is flight, but they are also important for providing insulation, camouflage, hearing, water repellency, communication, support, and a host of other functions. The large outer feathers on owls, the leading edge (the portion that faces the wind) and the trailing edges of the wings are both serrated. The serrations break up the wind, adding to the silent flow of air over them. When air blows over a smooth surface, as in a musical instrument, it creates sound, while the feathers with serrations break up sound allowing near-silent flight. The wings themselves have a velvety texture that is unique to owls and adds to their silent flight.

According to the Audubon Society, "The sound-dampening structures didn't evolve by chance. Silent flight is crucial for many owls' survival, and two long-held hypotheses attempt to explain this ability. The "stealthy hunting hypothesis" holds that owls fly inaudibly so that prey cannot hear them coming and have less time to escape. On the flip side, the "prey detection hypothesis" poses that silent flight aids owls in hearing and tracking prey. If you are trying to navigate to your next meal, like a mouse or vole scuttling quietly along the ground in the dark, you do not want your noisy wing beats impeding your hearing ability.".

The literature I have read suggests that Burrowing Owls, since they are diurnal (hunt during the day), do not need the ability to fly silently as their prey can see them coming, so they lack the fringing other owls possess. Other literature describes the feathers of Burrowing Owls and how their unique structure allows them to fly silently. Figure 12, the photo of the Burrowing Owl's feathers shows definite fringing on the trailing edge (lower edge) of the wing but barely visible fringing on the leading or upper edge. What I know is that I have often experienced Burrowing Owls flying over my head or near me in complete silence.

Compared to other owls, Burrowing Owls have long legs that allow them to run after prey, but they are also good flyers. Their wingspan is 19 to 23 inches (50-60cm) long, and given that they are only 7-9 inches tall, their wings are over twice the size of their height. This wingspan helps them fly slower and flap their wings less, which causes less turbulence and adds to their silent flight. I have seen a video of a barn owl flying across a big container of down feathers. As the owl flies over the feathers, the down feathers barely move.

Interestingly enough, feathers are essential for hearing. The iconic Great Horned Owl has tufts of feathers at the top of its head that are thought to be ears, but they are not ears and have nothing to do with hearing. On the other hand, the feathers of the Barn Owl's face, with its heart-shaped facial disk, have everything to do with hearing. The Barn Owls' unique arrangement of feathers and muscles can change the disk's shape, directing sound to the owl's ears. The facial disk is also slightly off center, allowing the owl to detect where the sound is coming from. These adaptations provide the Barn Owl with the most acute hearing of all owls.

Krista Le Piane, a graduate student at the University of California, Riverside, conducted research and found that "diet was a significant factor in how silent the flight is. Owls with a diet of mammals have developed good hearing and have also developed comb-like feather structures that allow silent flight. Owls that primarily eat insects and fish do not have as acute hearing and have less well-developed feather and wing structures that allow silent flight. Her research showed that a Burrowing Owl has very few comb-like structures, as the owls she studied were insect eaters. She also noted that Burrowing Owls she studied hunted during the day when they do not need acute hearing".

Her research most likely took place in California with the Burrowing Owl's western sub-species. The Western Burrowing Owl differs from the Florida Burrowing Owl, and diet may be one of these differences. In my experience, yes, "our" Burrowing Owls eat insects, but they eat a lot of mice, frogs and snakes, and anoles, and they hunt at night. I have a night vision camera monitoring the owls living on my front lawn. During the night, I see them flying in and out of the burrow, and in the morning, I often see frogs or small snakes in front of the burrow that were not present the previous day. Burrowing Owls are opportunistic eaters, so whatever is the most prevalent food source in the area will become the main diet of the owl. I am not a biologist and am not basing my observations on scientific observations, but just on what I observe. It would be interesting to conduct that same study on the Florida Burrowing Owls and see if there is a difference in feather structure because of diet.

Having owls living on my front lawn puts my husband and me in close contact with the owls. When my husband walks our dogs at night, the owl has great fun with him. The owl sits at the side of the road and waits. When my husband walks by the owl, it comes flying silently over his head, then screeches loudly, scaring the life out of him. On my husband's way back from the walk, the owl waits on the other side of the street, repeating this fun game. My husband comes in and says, "Dang, that owl did it to me again!!! Serrated wing edge or not, you cannot hear the Burrowing Owl flying overhead until it is in front of you.

Preening

Keeping feathers in good condition is vital for survival, and as the feathers harbor bacteria and parasites, they require regular care. Without a suitable set of feathers, an owl cannot fly, find food, escape predators, or regulate its temperature, so preening becomes a full-time job. Self-preening and mutual preening behaviors are frequently observed.

FIGURE 13 PREENING IN ADULT BURROWING OWLS AND YOUNG CHICKS

They use their beaks as a comb to re-align, clean, and remove parasites from the feathers. Burrowing Owls are frequently seen balanced on one foot, vigorously scratching their heads with their talons, with their beaks buried far under their wings, nibbling at their wings, stretching their wings, or smoothing their feathers with their beaks. These are all forms of preening behaviors. The owls get help from a sibling or a parent for the places they cannot reach. Mutual preening is often seen among many family members, resembles very romantic encounters, and presents itself as interesting Kodak® moments.

Camouflage

When animals and birds have the same color as their habitat, it allows them to blend in with their environment. This is true with Burrowing Owls, whose coloring serves as a highly effective camouflage. Their sandy coloring blends in with the sandy soil where they live. Besides the sand, these vacant lots are home to a wide variety of invasive weeds and native plants. During the winter, an invasive weed called Pusley (aka Florida snow) blankets our lawns and vacant lots. Despite its terrible name and invasive nature, Pusley has pretty purple flowers. As seen in Figure 14, the owls' spots blend in with the Pusley, making the owls extremely hard to see. So often, the only thing that gives their presence away is their bright yellow eyes and their swiveling heads. Often, I try to point out a Burrowing Owl, and it will take a bit of time for someone to finally see the owl; it is so well hidden in the vegetation.

FIGURE 14 CAMOUFLAGED OWL IN PUSLEY

Coloring

There is a distinct difference between the summer and winter plumage and male and female plumage in some bird species, but this is not true of the Burrowing Owl. Males spend considerable time outside the burrow protecting

31

the entrance, so the feathers become bleached by the sun. If you look at a single pair of owls, the female often appears darker in color than the male. However, young males and males with newly replaced feathers may appear darker, so this coloring difference is not a reliable field mark. Figure 16 shows a dark-colored female along with a lighter-colored male. Often the only way to tell the males and females apart is by behavior. The male stands guard in front of the burrow, while the female owl stays in the burrow or away from the entrance.

FIGURE 15 FRIENDLY KISS OR PREENING?

FIGURE 16 MALE AND FEMALE COLORING DIFFERENCE

Nestlings are born whitish-gray and gradually take on their parents' coloring. As juveniles, they have a telltale buff-colored chest and lack the adults' barring. In a few months, they grow to adult size, making them difficult to distinguish from the adults if it were not for the coloring difference from the adults.

FIGURE 18 ADULT (LEFT) VS JUVENILE (RIGHT) COLORING

Flight

When the Burrowing Owl chicks are born, they have a face only a mother could love. Their beaks are almost as big as their heads, and they are covered with a dense grayish white down that is especially important to keep them warm. They have buds for wings and cannot fly. But they grow rapidly, and within the first two weeks, they start their first molt, and start to develop feathers. Their wings are beginning to develop, and they are starting to look like a Burrowing Owls.

Figure 19 Adult wingspan

Watching the young birds from birth to fledging (the ability to fly and leave the nest) is wonderful and hilarious. Burrowing Owls lay their eggs over several days, so the young hatch over several days. The year I had seven chicks on my front lawn, the owls were three distinct sizes. This results in them learning to fly at different rates. Watching the chicks learning to fly is, in my opinion, better than watching the TV show Dancing with the Stars. At about a month of age, their wings are fully developed but not strong enough to fly, so they run around the yard flapping their wings to build up strength. Quickly the wings develop and are nearly twice as wide as they are tall. Then one day, they get a little air and get inches off the ground, probably scaring themselves to death. Next thing you know, they are flying for short distances, resulting in many collisions! When they finally gain enough strength to get off they ground, they must master the art of landing, which can be more complicated than flight. They often land on each other's heads or fall into the burrow, disappearing from view. It is very funny to watch.

At about 45 days, they are fully fledged, meaning they are capable of flight and look as though they have been doing it all their lives. At this point, they have a full complement of feathers and look very much like their parents.

Molting

Feathers are made of keratin, just like our fingernails, and since they are not a living substance must be shed and replaced when they become old and worn. This process is called molting. Molting in adults occurs after the young have fledged and the demands on the adults aren't as great. The flight feathers are usually replaced first. Molting follows a systematic pattern and may take 3-4 years for some of the larger owls to complete. This long duration of the molt is dramatic in the Bald Eagle. Juvenile Bald Eagles have black heads, but over 4-5 years, each successive yearly molt brings out more of the iconic white head. The brilliant white head is only seen when the eagle is about five years of age.

If the bird is not getting enough food, it will not have enough fat stores for thermoregulation, so it needs its feathers to keep warm or cool.

Weather also plays a role in molting, as extremely warm or cold weather can delay the process.

FIGURE 20 NEWLY HATCHED CHICKS

Goose-down pillows are one of the softest, most comfortable pillows made. Down feathers that the pillows are made from are the insulating feathers nearest the goose's body that help regulate its temperature. Burrowing Owl chicks are also born with downy feathers (above) that help keep them warm in the first few days of life. They grow quickly and start to lose the downy feathers, replacing them with their juvenile plumage. This usually occurs when they first leave the burrow within 10-14 days.

CHAPTER 6 Do You Know?

On August 16, 1916, with the signing of the Migratory Bird Treaty, the United States and Great Britain (on behalf of Canada) adopted a uniform system of protection for nearly all migratory bird species that inhabit and often migrate to the United States and Canada. It is one of the oldest wildlife protection laws on the books. The National Audubon Society fought hard to get this law passed and has worked through the years to keep it in existence and improve its scope. It has no doubt saved billions of birds over the years.

The Migratory Bird Treaty Act makes it illegal to "take, possess, import, export, transport, sell, purchase, barter, or offer for sale, purchase, or barter, any migratory bird, or the parts*, nests, or eggs of such a bird except under the terms of a valid Federal permit." Since this treaty was enacted, treaties have been established with Mexico, Japan, and Russia. Thus, if the Federal Migratory Bird Act Treaty protects a bird, it is illegal to possess its feathers. There is a $500.00 fine and jail time of up to 60 days if you are in possession of such a feather. Although the Burrowing Owls of Cape Coral do not migrate, the ones living in Western Canada do, so all Burrowing Owls are protected by this act.

If you find a feather on the ground, it is best to leave it there to avoid being fined or facing the remote possibility of contracting Avian Flu from the feather. If you know that it is from a bird not covered by this law, such as a starling or certain ducks, then it is all right to put it in your hat. Be sure the feather is not from a Bald Eagle. The fine for killing a Bald Eagle or even possessing its feather is $250,000 and 2 years in prison! Only full American Indians are permitted to have eagle feathers for ceremonial purposes.

Play it safe. Do not pick up feathers in the wild.

CHAPTER 7 Skeletal System

The most challenging part of writing this book was organizing the content. It was difficult to avoid being redundant when describing a Burrowing Owl's anatomy and physiology, as owls are incredibly well-oiled machines. They have evolved to fly and hunt, and nearly every aspect of their anatomy works in synchrony with each other system towards this goal. Here is a little on the anatomy and physiology of the Burrowing Owl.

The Skull

FIGURE 20 BURROWING OWL SKULL

Most owls, especially those that hunt at night, have an asymmetrical skull with asymmetrical ear openings that give them precision hearing. Since the Burrowing Owls hunt during daylight hours, they have minimal asymmetry.

The eye sockets in the skull are large to accommodate the owl's large eyes, which nearly take up the entire skull. The Burrowing Owl has no external ears, only skull openings that allow sound to enter. Looking into an owl's ears, you can see the owl's eyes. The skull in Figure 20 was given to me by one of the city maintenance workers who found this deceased owl remains in an advanced state of decomposition.

Bones

Licensed under the terms of the GNU Free Documentation
License Version 1

FIGURE 21 TYPICAL BIRD SKELETON

It was amazing to learn that the weight of the Burrowing Owls' bones is less than the weight of their feathers. Birds have a very lightweight yet strong skeletal system with crisscrossing reinforcement structures. This allows them to fly with minimal energy expense and overcome the stresses they face when flying and landing. The interior of a bird's larger bones is designed differently from that of humans. The owl's bones are not solid but are part of the respiratory system and contain air sacs that help pump air through to the lungs. Their entire skeletal system is designed for flight as well as the respiratory system.

Overall, birds have fewer bones than mammals and reptiles. This skeletal system's schematic shown below is not that of the Burrowing Owl but the generalized structure of all birds. The chest cavity's boney structure is similar in design to that of a human, with ribs and a sternum called the pectoral (shoulder) girdle, both of which serve as structures for muscle attachment and the attachment of the wings. In birds, however, the sternum is much larger, allowing for the attachment of more muscles.

Spinal Column

One of the big misconceptions about owls is that they can spin their heads all the way around. This is physically impossible. Owls can turn their heads 270 degrees, and at such a speed, it looks as though they are turning their heads all the way around. If we tried to replicate the movement of an owl's head, we would be flat on the floor, passed out, or worse, suffering from a traumatic neck injury. So how do the owls do this? It took the unlikely combination of an artist and a physician to discover how owls can turn their necks to such a degree. Until 2013, no one knew much about the blood flow to the owl's brain. It was known that owls have 14 vertebrae in the neck, twice as many as humans, allowing them to rotate their heads to a greater degree than humans, but something had to be different.

The Beak

Specialized structures called bristles are found around the owl's beak. These bristles help keep the owl's face clean as they are easier to clean than feathers. It is thought that these bristles can also act as sensory structures. Burrowing Owls also use their beaks to help dig their ten-foot-long burrows. The beak is also pointed downward to improve the aerodynamic flow of air while flying.

FIGURE 22 THE BEAK SHOWING BRISTLES

Talons

FIGURE 23 CLOSE-UP OF SHARP TALONS

Burrowing Owls have two toes that face forward and two that face backward. Scientifically, this is called a "zygodactyl" foot, and this arrangement gives the owl excellent stability. Two of the toes are movable, so when the owls have three toes facing forward and one backward, the arrangement is called" anisodactyl." This position gives the owls excellent holding power when aided by the needle-like talons at the ends of the toes. Besides the sharp talons, the foot's underside is rough-textured, adding another mechanism to hold prey.

You will often see the owls standing on one leg. I do not know why they do this; nothing is mentioned in the literature. They have quite a sense of balance and can be seen swaying in the breeze on one leg on a windy day without falling over.

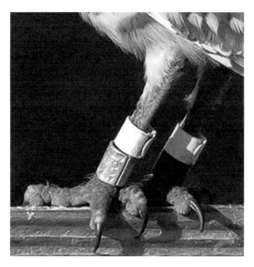

FIGURE 24 A BANDED BURROWING OWL

While the owl's auditory and visual capabilities allow it to locate and pursue its prey, the talons and beak of the owl do the final work. The owl kills its prey using these talons to crush the skull and knead the body. An owl's talons' crushing power varies according to prey size and the type and by the owl's size.

The talons are very sharp and are also used to defend themselves. Researchers place bands on birds' legs to track and study diet, reproduction rates, longevity, and more.

CHAPTER 8 The Senses

Hearing

Besides excellent eyesight, owls also have excellent hearing, as their entire head is designed to facilitate their hearing. This is partially because of the feathers on their face and partly due to their ears' position. Auditory neuroscientists have been studying barn owls because of their unique ability to locate sounds at night, during the day, or even under snow. Much of the information regarding the hearing in owls on the Internet is generalized for owls. It doesn't specifically mention Burrowing Owls, but Burrowing Owls certainly have incredible hearing, as do other owls.

Owls' ears are at the sides of their heads, much like humans but lack an external structure, and their ear openings are not symmetrically located. One ear is slightly lower than the other, which accounts for their incredible hearing abilities. Sounds reach an owl's ears at separate times, giving them the ability to pinpoint the sound's location. Even a millionth of a second difference is enough to let them determine the location of their prey. Once they receive that milli-second sound, they turn their heads until the sound reaches their ears simultaneously, locating their target.

Many owls have densely packed feathers in front of their ears, forming a circular pattern called a ruff that gathers sound. The wide range of television stations we enjoy often comes via a TV dish on our roof. This dish concentrates television signals and allows us to get many stations beamed by satellites high overhead. An owl's face is shaped like a satellite dish and designed to gather sound, giving them ten times better hearing than ours. Have you ever placed your hands behind your ears to try and hear something better? Putting your cupped hands behind your ears to listen to a sound makes the sound much louder. The ruff serves the same purpose, and muscles can change the ruff's shape to gather sounds as needed. As the ruff changes shape, there can be a 20 percent decibel difference in hearing. In addition to the owl's ability to regulate the ruff's shape, it is shaped differently in different owls depending on when they hunt. The Burrowing Owl ruff is relatively symmetrical since it is a diurnal owl and hunts during the day's lighter hours. Owls that hunt at night have ruffs that are asymmetrical and have better hearing than their day-hunting partners.

The feathers around the ear openings serve to protect the ear openings, diminish air turbulence when flying, and still allow sound waves to enter the ear canal. If you look into a human's ear, you see the eardrum. If you look into an owl's ear, you see the actual eye structure.

Thanks to the owl's excellent vision, acute hearing, specialized feathers, and talons, the saying "quiet as a mouse" is no defense against these "terrors of the night"!

Taste and Smell

Great Horned Owls will capture and eat a skunk. It has long been believed that owls do not have a sense of smell or taste. If they did, how could they hunt skunks?

New scientific study methods are being looked at to prove that owls do have a sense of smell. The jury is out on this quandary for now, but since their other senses are so acute, they do an excellent job of hunting even if they cannot smell. As far as I know, Burrowing Owls do not eat skunks, so do they have a sense of taste or smell? There is nothing in the literature for or against the answer to this question.

Sounds

One of the fun things to do with a small child is to ask them to make sounds of various animals. What does a pig do? "Oink." What does a cow do? Moooo. What does the owl do? Hoot! Cape Coral Burrowing Owls don't hoot, nor do any of the many sub-species of the Burrowing Owl.

They have quite an array of vocalizations, but many of them are rarely heard. The most common sound it makes is the male's coo-coo call when looking for a mate. At the beginning of the mating season, the males start to look for a mate if they do not already have one. This is also when the northerners come to Florida to escape the snow and cold weather. Remember that Cape Coral has over 400 miles of canals, so our homes are laid out to take advantage of the water access. Our living areas and master bedrooms most often face the canals, while less-used rooms like guest rooms face the front of the house. During the winter, the temperature is usually a pleasant 70-80°, air-conditioners are not used, and we leave windows open. My guest room windows are about

CAPE CORAL BURROWING OWLS DON'T HOOT

20 feet from the Burrowing Owl's burrow on my front lawn. The first year we had a male burrowing owl show up at our newly installed burrow, he called all night for a mate, and I mean ALL NIGHT! Coo-Coo-ooo, Coo-Coooooo, over and over again. My house guests and neighbors were ready to shoot the owl and me! Night after night, this repeated until he finally found a mate, and then all was quiet.

Another frequent sound is the alarm call. If you get too close to the burrow, the owl will let out a series of screeches to keep you away. This call is more intense when there are chicks in or around the burrow.

The young chicks have the most annoying (to me) "eep" call that they do regularly. I imagine the male may find it annoying, too, as sometimes he is seen off in the distance from the burrow, maybe to escape the noise. We have one owl site in town where the owls have dug burrows on both sides of a road. They use both burrows, and you never know in which burrow you will find them. But during nesting season, they choose one of the burrows, where the eggs are laid. When the chicks are old enough to be out of the burrow, they hop around constantly, making that "eep" call. At this site, the male is lucky because he flies across the street to the other burrow and stands on the t-perch, still close enough to watch his burrow but far enough away not to hear the noisy "kids."

The chicks can make a sound like a rattlesnake, serving as a defense call and can help keep predators away. I have never been close enough to hear this sound.

One day, I was doing some gardening near the burrow on my lawn and not paying attention to the owls on my front lawn. Three of the chicks were outside the burrow, along with one adult. I heard the adult make a clicking sound and saw the smallest chick run into the burrow. The adult made the same noise again, louder, and more forceful, and the second chick ran into the burrow. The third chick seemed to be a bit defiant and remained outside, so the adult made a very loud, repeated clicking sound that sent the third chick scurrying back into the burrow. I guess I was getting too close for comfort for the adult, and that was the alarm call to "get back in the burrow- NOW!". It just took a little extra effort to get the oldest chick back into the burrow.

CHAPTER 9 The Eyes

FIGURE 25 BACK EYES IN A BURROWING OWL

Burrowing Owls with black eyes??? I have devoted an entire chapter to the Burrowing Owls' eyes as I find birds' eyes fascinating. One of the first things people comment on about Burrowing Owls is their huge, beautiful yellow eyes. But the Burrowing Owls of Florida have unique eye coloring ranging from lemon yellow to nearly jet black. Just like humans, Burrowing Owls have forward-facing eyes that give them binocular vision. This allows them to see height, depth, and width in three dimensions. Binocular vision allows the owls to judge distance, making them highly accurate hunters, especially at night.

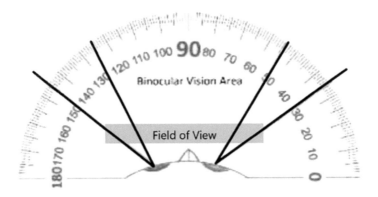

FIGURE 26 RANGE OF BINOCULAR VISION

Owls have a field of view of about 110°, which is what they can see looking straight ahead (outer lines in compass figure), and about 70% of that binocular, which is the ability of both eyes to see an object simultaneously. (The inner lines of the compass figure)

In studying the eyes of other species of birds, scientists found that the size of the eyes is proportional to the size of the bird. With raptors and owls, this is quite different. They have exceptionally large eyes relative to their size. This size difference is expected as they rely heavily on their ability to see for hunting.

The owl's acute vision that has evolved over millions of years (remember, owls have been around that long!) has played a big part in the structure of the eye itself. As the eyes got larger and larger, they took up more and more of the cranial cavity causing the eyes to be compressed. Compression became so extreme that owls now have tubular eyes that do not rotate like ours but are fixed in their heads. Most birds have structures called sclerotic rings that hold the eyes in place. These sclerotic rings are much more prominent in owls, and it is interesting to note that when an owl dies in the wild, these sclerotic rings are still in place after the rest of the body decomposes or is eaten by other animals.

Cornea

The first structure in the eye is the cornea. This is the transparent covering of the eye and serves as the eye's first lens. It controls and focuses light as it enters the eye. As light comes into the eye, the cornea refracts (bends) the light onto the eye's lens. This structure is like the cornea in the human eye.

Iris

The iris is a muscular diaphragm that controls the pupil's diameter and size, thus regulating the amount of light that enters the eye. The iris determines eye color. Owls with dark or black eyes, such as the Barred Owl, hunt at night, helping them blend in at night. Owls with orange eyes, such as the Snowy Owl and the Great Horned Owl, are active at dusk and dawn (crepuscular), and owls with yellow eyes, like the Burrowing Owls, are diurnal, which means they hunt during the day.

The Burrowing Owls of Florida do not seem to fit into this eye coloring scheme. They indeed have brilliant yellow eyes and do hunt during the day. I have a night vision camera on my front lawn and can observe the owls flying in and out of the burrow at night. I have seen them flying in with what seems to be insects and larger prey, and I see frogs, lizards, and other small food bits at the entrance to the burrow early in the morning, so I know they are hunting at night. One night around 3:00 am, I had the remote camera zoomed in on the burrow entrance. A dead mouse dropped from out of camera range in front of the burrow, where it remained for a while. Suddenly, an owl, presumed to be the female, flew out of the burrow, grabbed the mouse, and flew off with it.

Over the years, here in Florida, we have seen Burrowing Owls with eye colorings other than yellow. Their eye coloring ranges from muddy yellow to nearly black and everything in between. We even see Burrowing Owls with very dark eyes and yellow specks scattered throughout the iris. This abnormal eye coloring is thought to be due to a recessive gene. Cape Coral and Florida's owls do not migrate and do not usually venture far from where they were born. Thanks to the banding of birds, biologists can track mating, and they suspect that inbreeding is the cause of the unusual variations in eye coloring.

About 15 years ago, Pascha Donaldson, then president of Cape Coral Friends of Wildlife, the organization that helps protect the Burrowing Owl in Cape Coral, discovered an owl with one yellow eye and one black eye. At that time, we were not sure if the owl had an injured eye, but we began seeing more and more owls with these unusually colored eyes over the years.

Following the information noted above concerning the relationship between eye color and hunting habits, when do these guys hunt? This unusual eye coloring is considered a genetic variation and, apparently, not seen in the Burrowing Owl's western subspecies.

I had heard that a photographer had submitted a photograph he had taken of one of these dark-eyed owls to a photo contest. The judges rejected his photo because they thought his photo was altered with Photoshop®. Figure 27, is the most unusual Burrowing Owl in the world, having one yellow eye and one dark eye. Also, figure 27 is of two other unique owls, one with crystal eyes and another with totally black eyes.

FIGURE 27 BI-COLORED EYES, CRYSTAL EYES AND BLACK EYES

Pupil

The pupil is the opening in the center of the iris that allows light to enter the eye. The larger the pupil, the more light enters; conversely, the smaller the pupil, the less light enters the eye. As seen in Figure 28, Burrowing Owls have huge pupils, which gives them excellent night vision.

FIGURE 28 PUPIL SIZE

Retina

Like humans, the retina is located at the back of the eye. It focuses light that has entered the eye, converts that light to signals, and transmits the signal to the brain for processing into an image. Many nocturnal animals have a thin membrane behind the retina called the tapetum lucidum. This structure reflects light back through the retina, giving owls (as well as many other animals) even more light for night vision. This shows up as "eye shine" in animals and differs from "red-eye which is just light reflecting off the blood vessels on the retina.

FIGURE 29 RED EYE   FIGURE 29-A EYE SHINE

Eyelids

Burrowing Owls, all other owls and raptors, and many mammals have three eyelids. Like humans, the upper eyelid moves downward and is used for blinking, and the lower one moves upward when the owl sleeps. A third eyelid, the nictitating membrane, is shown in the owl in Figure 30. It moves across and moistens the eyes while still allowing the owl to see.

FIGURE 30 BURROWING OWL WITH THIRD EYELID SHOWING.

Parallax

FIGURE 31 HEAD TILT IN JUVENILES

CAPE CORAL BURROWING OWLS DON'T HOOT

The ability to judge distance comes from a phenomenon called parallax. Look at an object on a wall in front of you. Without moving your head, alternately open and close your right eye and then your left eye. The movement of your eyes gives the appearance that the object is changing position on the wall. This is because you are looking at it from a different point of view with each eye change. Using both eyes is what gives us the ability to judge distance. People who have lost vision in one eye have difficulty driving because they lose depth perception and the ability to judge distance.

Juvenile Burrowing Owls need to learn this skill. Since their eyes do not move in their heads, they must turn their entire head to get a different view of you and determine how far away you are. When the chicks learn this skill, it is one of the cutest things you have ever seen. Since they have those extra vertebrae in their necks and are flexible, they can turn their heads 180° upside down! This makes for some adorable photos.

CHAPTER 10 Reproduction

Mate Selection

According to the Florida Fish and Wildlife Conservation Commission (FWCC), the official nesting season is from February 15 through July 10. The juvenile males from the spring clutch are sexually mature by late fall and in early winter start looking for a burrow to claim their own. They may dig a new burrow or take over an abandoned burrow. Nothing much happens from November through January. Burrowing Owls mate for life, so if a pair has survived the summer together, they could have a second clutch over the winter, as occasionally we have seen chicks as early as November.

As February approaches, the unpaired males start looking for a mate, as described in the chapter on sounds. Thanks to the tagging of the Burrowing Owls by biologists, they have noted that even though the owls mate for life, owls have exhibited polygamous behavior. If mating isn't successful or the male proves unworthy, the female may choose a new mate. Since they do not migrate and, for the most part, do not travel very far from where they are born, there is not a big gene pool from which they can choose a mate, so the females cannot be too picky. Selecting a mate and mating undoubtedly depends on many factors, such as weather, plumage, food availability, habitat, and mate availability.

By the beginning of the nesting season, the male has laid claim to his burrow. David Johnson, Director of the Global Owl Project, said that the male Burrowing Owl have "everything invested in his burrow because it is everything he has." If he loses his burrow, he loses everything. The male is a vital part of the nesting process and needs to prove that he can be a good provider for the female and the family".

Decoration

FIGURE 32 DECORATION BY A MALE BURROWING OWL

Towards the end of February, the City of Cape Coral and Cape Coral Friends of Wildlife gets telephone calls from angry citizens, yelling and screaming, "my owls, arrest them, who could do such a thing", and more. When they finally calm down and can speak coherently, they report that they woke up to find garbage all over "their" burrow. On their walks, the burrow on an empty lot they pass every morning has trash all over the burrow entrance. Who would do such a thing, they ask? "I want a full-scale investigation". We try to explain that the owl is bringing this trash to the burrow. The caller protests, "no, there is a whole t-shirt; an owl can't carry that!" Well, apparently, he can and did! The caller is shocked and amazed to discover that the male owl brought all that trash to the burrow to get ready for the nesting season. has begun is that the male starts to "decorate", a sure-fire signal that the nesting process has begun. Little is known about this process, but it is undoubtedly one of the more fascinating and quirky aspects of a Burrowing Owl's life. The male begins to collect anything he can find and brings it to the burrow (and he is known to fly up to a half-mile away to steal decoration from another male's burrow). He brings items to line the burrow's chamber where the eggs are laid, and the rest is spread around the outside of the burrow.

The collection of things that are brought to the burrow is nothing short of amazing. We have found hamburger wrappers, tube socks, entire t-shirts, cigarette butts, jelly donuts, crab legs, bank receipts, surgical gloves, dog leashes, kids' homework, stuffed animals, flowers, and many other interesting things. One biologist studying the owls found two pairs of lace ladies' silk underwear at a burrow, one red and one blue. That had to be the most unusual! Some burrows are sparsely decorated, and others have the entire burrow entrance covered. The older and more experienced the male, the more decorated the burrow.

David Thomas of the Global Owl Project studies the Burrowing Owl's Western sub-species and finds that those owls prefer red, white, blue, and green items and stay away from grey and black. One year the owl on my front lawn brought gray duct tape to the burrow. Perhaps something needed repair in the burrow, or is this color choice is another variation between the Western and Florida sub-species? Who knows?

One morning I found a dishtowel in front of the burrow at my house. Now a dish towel in it itself is not interesting, but where he got the towel generates a lot of interest. "My owl" went on to my neighbor's boat and took his lucky fishing towel. The owl brought the towel to the burrow and practiced what I call Owl Feng Shui. The owl moved it around for three nights until he finally settled on a spot near the burrow entrance. The owls leave this decoration at the burrow site until the chicks are about six weeks old, and then it is removed. I want to think it is recycled, but I have no idea what the owls do with the decoration, and none of the literature mentions its disposal.

Each year I give an "award" to the best-decorated burrow. One year, Cape Elementary School got the award for having the most varied candy wrapper collection. The owls had the most extensive collection of candy wrappers I had ever seen. Kindness Animal Hospital West got the most monochromatic design award as the owls found tissues and looked like it snowed around the burrow. The 2021 award went to the owls who were following CDC (Centers for Disease Control) Covid-19 guidelines. Not only did they have two burrows about six feet away from each other practicing social distancing, but I found a disposable mask at the burrow too!

In addition to these exciting treasures, the owls also bring animal feces to the burrow. The feces, or dung, is used to line the nesting chamber and alert other males that the burrow is occupied but serves different purposes. Several studies have been done to determine why the owl exhibits this behavior.

A study by Ryan S. Brady from Boise State University proposed several hypotheses about why dung is brought to the burrow.

"Anti-predation: Dung masks the scent of owls and their nest contents and thus deters terrestrial predators.

Optimal microclimate: Dung creates a more suitable burrow microenvironment for adult owls and their developing young.

Thermal insulation

Reducing relative humidity within nest chambers

Reducing levels of carbon dioxide within nest chambers

Anti-ectoparasite: Dung reduces ectoparasite loads on adult and nestling owls."

Brady did his studies on the Burrowing Owls' western subspecies, so his findings may or may not apply to the Cape Coral Burrowing Owls. His studies came up with some interesting discoveries, such as the fact that the amount of dung had little correlation with the predation level, but the more dung in the burrow, the lower the concentration of carbon dioxide in the nest chamber. Interestingly, Burrowing Owls have a high tolerance for carbon dioxide since their nest chambers are so far from the entrance, and little air movement occurs. Apparently, the dung collection is an adaptation to reduce carbon dioxide levels in the burrow. He found, however, that it does not affect the number of fleas found on the owls either.

The Owl may use the dung to collect dung beetles or other insects to use as food. Studies from the University of Florida showed that burrows with a large amount of dung showed a large amount of beetle remains in the regurgitated pellets at the burrow site. They couldn't determine if the owls were intentionally using the dung to attract food, but since owls are notoriously wise, who knows?

It is also thought that the dung is used to teach young chicks how to hunt. As insects gather on the feces, the chicks can hone their hunting skills close to home and can quickly duck back into the burrow if they are in danger.

Egg Production

The female can lay up to a dozen smooth white eggs about an inch long and incubate them for 28 days and the eggs are laid over several days. She spends most of her time in the burrow while the male provides most of the food. She has been observed to have a brooding pouch that keeps the eggs warm. The brooding pouch is a hollowed-out area in her abdomen where she removes some feathers to create a pouch that keeps the eggs and the young hatchlings warm as she sits on them. In Florida, the eggs can stay warm in the burrow even without her sitting on the eggs, allowing the female to leave the burrow for some r & r and to hunt. At about 28 days, the eggs begin to hatch, and just as the eggs were laid over several days, the eggs hatch over several days.

FIGURE 33 BURROWING OWL EGGS

FIGURE 34 RANGE OF MATURATION IN SINGLE BROOD

The photo above shows a family of Burrowing Owls. The adult is at the extreme left. This is a perfect example of how fast chicks grow. With the oldest chicks in the back, the middle chicks on the front right, and the youngest in the front still showing its downy feathers.

CHAPTER 11 Growth and Development

Leaving the protected environment of an egg is a complicated process for a Burrowing Owl. Nature provides the developing embryo with an egg tooth structure, a protrusion on the top of the beak that allows the chick to crack open

the egg. This egg tooth usually falls off several days after the chick is born. The hatching process takes place over several days, just as the laying of the eggs did at the start.

Interestingly, the year seven chicks successfully hatched on my front lawn; I noticed the chicks were three distinctly varied sizes. Since the chicks grow so fast and hatch over several days, this visible difference in size can be seen.

Early Life:

At birth, the owlets are covered with a greyish-white down. The firstborn's survival rate in a clutch is higher than the last-born chicks, which may die or be killed if there isn't enough food. Burrowing Owls make good parents. The young chicks usually stay with their parents through the spring and summer and learn the skills necessary to survive.

FIGURE 35 AGING OF JUVENILES

During that time, the parents are responsible for teaching them how to fly and hunt for themselves. They grow rapidly, and within a few days, they begin to develop feathers and wings. This collage photo, taken by a biologist, Tom Allen, shows the owlets at several stages of growth. Tom took the four outer photos, and I took the center photo. It is accepted knowledge in the biological community that the chicks emerged from the burrow at about two weeks of age. The outer photos show the chicks from age five-day to seven–nine-days to fourteen days old, and then a three-week-old. I took the center photo of two chicks on my front lawn. I looked out one day, and there were these two tiny chicks at the entrance to the burrow, obviously younger than two weeks of age. They must have taken a wrong turn and wandered out of the burrow. A day or two later, one of them again tried to leave the burrow too soon and got a stern look from Mom!

FIGURE 36 STERN LOOK FROM MOM

Chicks are fully fledged at a month and a half to two months of age, meaning they can fly and leave the parental nest. When developing their wings, they need to learn many skills to survive independently. Watching for predators must be instinctive, as I have observed the chicks looking towards the sky from the first day out of the burrow. I also observe the chicks learning to hunt as they run in brief spurts and then pounce, attempting to catch prey. As stated, they use the dung in front of the burrow as a hunting tool, catching the bugs the dung attracts.

Digging lessons must be on the agenda of things to learn. The year we had the seven chicks on my front lawn, I saw all seven chicks lined up in a semi-circle in front of the burrow. Suddenly, sand came flying out of the burrow entrance. Was the parent teaching them how to dig? Watching the little ones dodging the sand spraying all over them was fun. Of course, I did not have my camera handy for this Kodak® moment. The chicks stay around the burrow for the rest of the summer, waiting for fall when they are ready to start their own families.

CHAPTER 12 Habitat

Visitors ask how we became the "epicenter" of the Burrowing Owl population in Florida and possibly the world. The answer is location, location, location but more accurately, habitat, habitat, habitat.

There are approximately 220 species of owls globally, and the Burrowing Owls are the only owls that live underground. In the United States, there are two subspecies of Burrowing Owls, the western subspecies (Athene Cunicularia hypugia) and the Florida subspecies (Athene Cunicularia floridana).

Much of the literature states that Burrowing Owls prefer to live on prairies and in abandoned burrows dug by prairie dogs, armadillos, and other such wildlife. This is quite true for the Burrowing Owls' western subspecies, but not for the Florida Burrowing Owls. Because of our sandy soil and the fact that Florida has few ground-dwelling animals, our industrious little Burrowing Owls dig their burrows using their sharp talons and beaks. They scrape the ground, kicking the sand backward, where the excavated sand piles up in a mound by the entrance. They can dig a ten-foot-long burrow in just a few days. To visitors' enjoyment and amazement, we often see sand flying out of the burrow as the owls are cleaning or extending the burrow or just performing this genetic adaptation. This digging behavior makes our Florida Burrowing Owls unique.

Historically, the owls lived in the Central Plains area of Florida, but they followed natural disturbances such as occurred in Cape Coral and moved west, expanding their breeding range. Burrowing Owls prefer open areas with few trees and little ground vegetation.

When the bulldozers were done making a mess of Cape Coral, it was initially the perfect habitat for the owls. There were miles and miles of flat empty land with mostly soft sand where the owls could dig their burrows. The depth of the burrow depends mainly on the soil. It can be only inches deep to several feet below the surface. As was mentioned in an earlier chapter, some of our soil contains hard limestone deposits, so if an owl hits hard pack soil or coral, it changes direction. We can often tell the tunnel's general direction by the pile of excavated dirt at the burrow entrance. The opening into the burrow is about 4-6 inches in circumference, and the tunnel usually has a curve to keep the light down to a minimum, and at the end of the burrow is a chamber where the family lives and cares for the young. The chamber has a sandy floor, and the male brings grass and bits of paper or other "stuff" they find to line the floor. of the burrow where they raise their young.

CHAPTER 13 Development

Historically, Burrowing Owls have been found throughout the United States in open terrains such as prairies, low grasslands, deserts, farms, and ranches. Development, pesticides, predation, and human interaction have drastically reduced their range as prairie-like habitat has been cleared for human habitation. Here in Florida, massive tracts of land are being cleared for development as millions of northerners move south to retire in the warm sunshine. The Burrowing Owl is one of the few animals that benefit from man's habitat destruction, so the vast destruction of wetlands and woodland habitats that was to become Cape Coral was precisely the type of habitat the owls needed to survive.

The early development of Cape Coral left miles and miles of wide-open space for the owls. But as homes, schools, parks, and businesses are built, the empty lots that the owls rely on are being developed. Once, the owls were commonly found on vacant lots throughout the city, but as the number of lots is dwindling, the places the owls have available to choose for their burrows are also dwindling. The places that the owls now left to choose for their burrows can be mind-boggling. The burrows can be found in the highway medians, at the curbsides at living on busy street corner. school crossings, in the middle of busy parking lots, and on the edge of roads. Today it is common to find owls digging a burrow in the pile of sand destined to be fill for a new home or living in the drainage pipes that run under our driveways to allow water to flow to larger drainage pipes. David Johnson calls this "desperation housing," as there is little land left for the owls to use.

FIGURE 37 BURROWING OWLS AT CURBSIDE

The pair of owls in figure 37 live at the curb line of a very busy street and, according to the owner of the home, there have been owls living at that corner for nearly two decades. Here they are, watching the school bus go by as they do every morning.

I received a call from a photographer who wanted me to take him out to photograph the owls. He was precise in wanting to be "out of town" and have "good backgrounds." I told him he had better bring a boat because Cape Coral is a peninsula, and we do not have an "out of town." I then went to a prime example of desperation housing, where this pair of Burrowing Owls live near a school. I waited until a school bus went by, shot Figure 37, and sent it to him, telling him this is where the owls often live. I took him too much better places to get his pictures, and he was happy.

The photos in Figure 38 are prime examples of "desperation housing." A permit was obtained to do a burrow "take" to build this home. During the non-nesting season, the burrow was checked to ensure there were no "flightless young" in the burrow. If none are present, the burrow is closed, and construction begins on the house. Burrowing Owls have what is called "nest fidelity" and will try to return to their previous home if displaced or moved, which is precisely what these owls did. They returned home and began digging their burrow in the pile of sand in front of the home.

FIGURE 38 NEST FIDELITY IN BURROWING OWL
PHOTOS BY KIM BURCH

CHAPTER 14 Predators and Threats

Figure 39 Dangerous burrow in median of a roadway

Cars, cats, and humans are the biggest threats to Burrowing Owls. There is no doubt that habitat loss is the biggest threat to the Burrowing Owl, but other threats and predators take their toll on the owls.

Here in Cape Coral, the owls are notorious for picking some dangerous places to dig their burrow such as in the median of a major highway that runs through town, and many are at the side of a residential road. As you can imagine, living near cars takes its toll on young chicks when they are learning to fly. Another thing that is not in the Burrowing Owls' favor with cars is that, unlike other birds, Burrowing Owls fly down, not up. Looking at Figure 39, you can see how easy it is for an owl to get hit by a car returning to its burrow as it would be flying right in the path of that oncoming car returning to its burrow.

FIGURE 40 COOPERS HAWK

Hawks such as the Coopers Hawk pictured in figure 40 are another threat to the Burrowing Owls. While working with the owls, I have observed Coopers' Hawks standing on a PVC pipe near a burrow entrance, waiting for the owls to emerge.

As a side note, cats kill 2.4 billion birds each year in the United States alone, according to the American Bird Conservancy. Feral cats are a problem for all birds, and people do not realize that domesticated cats allowed to roam outside are just as big a problem. Burrowing Owls are small enough to be prey for a cat, and there are plenty of stray cats around the city to target the owls.

CHAPTER 15 Help! I've Found an Injured Owl

First off, do not think you will be a Good Samaritan and raise the owl or any other wildlife on your own. It is illegal to keep a Burrowing Owl and most wildlife species. Wildlife animals that are raised by their rescuer rarely survive. Leave wild animals in their natural habitat where they belong and will do better.

Determine if the owl or any wildlife is injured or actually needs rescuing. Visually check for obvious signs of injury, such as a broken wing, bleeding, shivering, or a dead parent nearby. Only if it has injuries or is in a compromised situation as these should a rescue be attempted.

Check the status of the feathers. If it has downy feathers and you know where the burrow or nest is, try to put the owlet back near the burrow or the bird back in the nest if you can reach it.

Occasionally, a parent will kick a bird out of a nest to encourage it to fly. Burrowing Owls will kick a chick out of the burrow if it is ill or if the parents cannot care for the young bird.

WEAR GLOVES when touching the owl or other wildlife.

Contrary to popular belief, the mothers will not reject the baby if humans have touched it. Leave the area if you are returning the owl to the burrow! If the mother sees you hanging around, she will not return to feed the baby. Observe from a safe distance. If the parents do not return or you have an injured owl, call:

C.R.O.W (239) 472-3644

Kindness Animal Hospital East (239) 945-0111 or West Office (239) 542-7387
Chiquita Animal Hospital (239) 945-2279

I frequently get phone calls from homeowners reporting an owl under the bushes in front of their homes. They tell me that the owl has been there for several days and does not appear to move. The last thing I do is run over to the house to check if the bird is injured. Instead, I tell them to wait until dusk or after dark and see if the owl is still there. I tell the homeowner that sitting under a bush like this is typical behavior, and there is probably nothing wrong with the owl. I tell them to be sure and call me back if they see the owl at night, and I will come out and check on the owl. I never get a return call.

The homeowners may or may not tell me that owls are living on their street, but the whereabouts of the burrows are usually unknown. This is just another of the strange behaviors of the Burrowing Owls.

FIGURE 40 CURIOUS JUVENILE

CHAPTER 16 Finding the Owls

Where Can I Find the Burrowing Owls?

Finding the owls is one of the most challenging things to put into this book because they are live creatures, moving and subject to predation. I could tell you where there is a burrow with a family of owls, and twelve hours later, the family could be wiped out by a hawk, a cat, or one of our monitor lizards, or they could have just plain moved. What is better is that you know what to look for and some resources available to help you find the owls.

FIGURE 42 TYPICAL BURROW SITE (MAY NOT HAVE A SIGN)

In 2021, owls could be found all over town in some of the most unusual places. If you go to the City of Cape Coral website, you can download a map of the sites where the owls can be found. This map is several years old, and the owls have abandoned some sites; however, the map is a big help.

Every known burrow that is located on an undeveloped lot is marked with four PVC pipes and a wooden T-perch. So, as you drive around Cape Coral, you will see what looks like crosses all over town, and you will find that these "crosses" do not mark terrible drivers, nor do we have a lot of pet cemeteries. They all mark Burrowing Owl burrows. This is where it gets interesting. The owl's favorite location to dig its burrow is one of the numerous empty lots we have in the city. But they are also found in parks (Camelot, Saratoga, and BMX Parks), at schools (Cape Elementary and Pelican Elementary), road medians (Veterans Parkway, Pelican Blvd., Country Club Blvd, in swales, (Cay West Shopping Center), and on private lawns. They are often only inches away from the edge of the road or curb, under portable basketball nets, or standing on someone's windowsill.

Figure 42 above is what a typical site looks like. Four PVC pipes and a t-perch marks a burrow site, and often you will see the owls standing on the perch. Not every burrow is marked with a sign attached to the T-perch. If you look carefully, you will see two Burrowing Owls standing on the top of the T-perch.

So, what's the big deal about finding them? First, Cape Coral is the second-largest city in Florida, covering over 100 square miles. Second, at the last count, which was well over 12 years ago, there were 2700 known burrows, and third, at only 7 to 9 inches tall, the Burrowing Owl is tiny and is a master at camouflage.

If you are coming from the Tampa area, I suggest looking at the city map and starting with the parks shown on that map in the city's northern part. If you are coming from Sanibel or the SW Regional Airport area, I suggest going to Pelican Ballfield. On your way to these sites, be sure and look for those 4 PVC pipes; you may get lucky and find an owl standing on the t-perch.

Pelican Ball field

FIGURE 43 PELICAN BASE BALL COMPLEX

Pelican ball field is part of the soccer and baseball field c omplex that is located at 4124 Pelican Blvd. is a sure bet to see owls. There are owls on all four sides of the park as of this writing. On 42nd Terrace, the south side of the park, numerous burrow sites are marked off with the PVC pipes, any of which may be occupied by an owl. Anywhere there is a wooden T-perch, there is a burrow entrance. That is where you should look for an owl.

If you are tech-savvy, have some fun with the Internet program Google Earth. If you put in 410 SW 42nd Terrace, Cape Coral, as a search in Google Earth and then use the street feature to look across the street from the house. You can see all the PVC pipes along the south side of the park. "walk" down the street and look at the wooden perches; sometimes, you can see an owl standing on a t-perch. That is so cool that you can see these owls from space.

Continue down 42nd Street and turn into the small parking lot at the end. Check for burrows in the grass on SW 5th Avenue. Another burrow is at the end of the parking lot, along the fence line. Check to see if it is active. Then turn right on SW 41st Street to another burrow along the ball field's fence line. A dirt path leads to the maintenance shed that you can use to get closer to a burrow located beside the fence line. This burrow was very close to a set of bleachers that were destroyed by Hurricane Ian and have not yet been replaced.

There is a new burrow at the park's northern exit near the children's playground, and finally, there is one on the eastern side of the ball field on Pelican Blvd; that may be active. To view this one, drive past the site, park in the parking lot, and walk back to the telephone pole where the burrow is located. Do not park on Pelican Blvd. Be sure to read the rules and regulations chapter so you do not get in trouble with the law!

Other Places to Find Owls

Is Cape Coral the only place you can find Burrowing Owls? The answer to that question is yes and no. If you search the app E-bird, you will find there have been sightings of Burrowing Owls throughout the State of Florida. But if the Burrowing Owl is on your life list, Cape Coral is the place to go to have the best success in checking it off your list. If you are staying in the Marco Island area, this is your second and next best place to see the owls. They have over 100 nesting pairs, and they too mark the burrows with PVC pipes.

If you are on the east coast of Florida and do not want to make the 3 1/2-hour trip across the state, check out Brian Piccolo Sports Park & Velodrome, located at 9501 Sheridan St., Cooper City, FL 33024. A small population of Burrowing Owls live at that park, and they are quite easy to find.

It has been reported to me that Burrowing Owls live on a golf course in Marathon in the Florida Keys. I believe the golf course is on Sombrero Blvd, but I am not positive about that location. Besides those four areas, your chances of seeing a Burrowing Owl in Florida are slim.

CHAPTER 17 Diet

FIGURE 44 BURROWING OWLS EATING AN ANOLE
AND AN INSECT. TOP PHOTO BY JACK HOLMES OF
BATON ROUGE LOUISIANA

When researching the eating habits, hunting habits, and diets of the Burrowing Owl, coupled with my observations of the Burrowing Owls living on my front lawn, it is apparent that they hunt for food any time they want. Most literature says they are diurnal, which means they hunt during the day. Having the owls on my front lawn and the ability to watch them at night with my infrared camera, I can watch them 24 hours a day. I see both male and female owls flying in and out of the burrow through the night and often find frogs, birds, snakes, and unidentified bits of flesh at the burrow entrance in the early morning. I also see them munching on an insect or some sort of prey they have captured during the day.

According to the Low Country Raptors Organization, they note that "Females do a lot of hunting during the day and catch invertebrates, while males hunt during the night and catch mostly vertebrates." People often ask me, "what do they eat"? Hands down, the favorite- food of the Burrowing Owl is a nice fat an Anole and an insect or a mouse. Second, on their list of foods is anything they can get their talons on as they are opportunist feeders. They will eat anoles (those little lizard-like creatures that are all over Florida), frogs, snakes, and toads and can capture a small bird that can be nearly their own size. Grasshoppers, beetles, moths, termites, dragonflies, caterpillars, and other insects are also on their menu. As a side note, having a Burrowing Owl living on your front lawn is free pest control. Add to that the large flocks of Ibis that wander our neighborhoods eating the underground insects.; you shouldn't need toxic herbicides on your lawns.

Burrowing Owls have long, featherless legs that allow them to run quite well. They are always on the lookout for opportunities for a good meal. If they spot prey, they will either silently swoop down on it, catching their prey in mid-air, or run along the ground towards their prey.

Nearly all Cape Coral homes are cinder block construction, so termite infestation is not a significant issue. The termite problem in Florida as a whole is a big issue, to where the University of Florida offers a 40-hour seminar just on termites. The Burrowing Owls' fondness for termites is another item on the list of reasons for having a Burrowing Owl living on your front lawn if your home is constructed of wood.

Digestion

FIGURE 45 OWL PELLET

Burrowing owls, as with all birds, do not have teeth. This lack of teeth may be an adaptation to reduce weight and aid flight, as teeth require a strong, heavy jawbone. The Burrowing Owl's food consists mainly of prey that they rip apart with their talons and beaks or eat whole. They have two stomachs, the proventriculus, which produces enzymes that start the digestive process, and the gizzard, a muscular structure that breaks up and grinds the food. The prey's fur, bones, and other indigestible parts are compressed into a pellet and passed back up into the proventriculus, where it is stored for up to ten hours before being coughed up. The owl cannot eat until the pellet is expelled. Pellets are especially useful to scientists who can dissect them and study an owl's diet.

The regurgitated pellet of a great horned owl is 2-3 inches long, but as Figure 45 shows, burrowing owl pellets are small (above). The small black circle seen on this pellet appears to be the beetle's shell.

As a side note, Burrowing Owls are unique because they can be seen at any time of the day. People looking for other owls usually do this at night or early evening, and they do this by looking for pellets on the ground. Pellets on the ground are a good sign that an owl is quietly sitting in a tree above their heads. Burrowing Owls are a lot easier to find as the male is sitting outside, guarding the burrow all day, all year long. Only during the sultry afternoon Florida sun do they sometimes hide to get out of the heat. Often you will see an owl standing behind the t-perch to get in its shadow, out of the sun.

CHAPTER 18 Conservation and Preservation

The Burrowing Owl is listed as endangered in Canada, Iowa, and Minnesota. It is a species of special concern in California, Idaho, Kansas, Montana, Nebraska,

Oklahoma, Oregon, South Dakota, Utah, and Washington. In 2018, the status of the Burrowing Owl in Florida was changed from a "species of special concern" to "threatened."

In 2014, the Audubon Society released a study that listed 314 birds that climate change will seriously threaten by the end of the century. A new study released in 2019 increased that number to 389 "birds on the brink" of losing at least half of their current ranges by the year 2080 because of climate change. The Burrowing Owl is on that list.

According to the North American Breeding Bird Survey, Cornell Labs reports that "Burrowing Owls are still numerous, but populations have declined by about 33% between 1966 and 2015." The Imperial Valley, home to nearly one-third of California's Burrowing Owl population, suffered a Burrowing Owl population decline of 27% IN ONE YEAR.

"Pesticides, collisions with vehicles, shooting, entanglement in loose fences and similar man-made hazards, and hunting by introduced predators (including domestic cats and dogs) are major sources of mortality. While Burrowing Owls have benefited from protective legislation, reintroduction and habitat protection programs, and artificial nest burrows. Because they do not require large uninterrupted stretches of habitat, these owls can benefit from the protection of relatively small patches of suitable land."

As stated, we do not know at this point (2021) how many Burrowing Owls we have in Cape Coral, nor do we know if the population is increasing or decreasing. Florida Fish and Wildlife Conservation Commission Conservation Commission (FWCC) surveyed the Burrowing Owls statewide to have the data to substantiate the change of status to threatened. There is a count in progress by Cape Coral Friends of Wildlife, but the final statistics will not be out for several more years. Judging from the 5-year studies done in the previous years that suggest the population is about 1000 nesting pairs, the new preliminary estimates put the population between 2500-3500 owls, the Burrowing Owls seem to be holding their own. As far as we know, we have not had a dramatic increase or decrease in the population.

CAPE CORAL BURROWING OWLS DON'T HOOT

With that said, where do we stand here in Cape Coral? There is no doubt that Cape Coral is growing. Forbes and national newspapers have ranked the Cape Coral/Fort Myers area as the fastest-growing region of the country in past years.

When Cape Coral was established, the projected population was set at 400,000 residents, based on having no high-rise buildings and primarily single-family homes. Somewhere along the line, that changed, and massive projects such as Tarpon Point and Cape Harbor were allowed, along with their multi-story buildings. The projected population projection was also moved up to 450,000 people.

How soon will Cape Coral reach critical mass? Granted, according to projections, we are only at half the projected population levels, but do we want a city with bumper to bumper traffic and wall-to-wall people, or did we come to Cape Coral to get out of that rat race? So many people say they like the west side of Florida much better because it is quieter and much less congested. Many of us came here because Cape Coral offered us that hometown atmosphere, even though it is such a large city. If you ask most of the residents, they will say they do not want Cape Coral to grow into a Miami of the West.

The Burrowing Owl is one of the greatest assets this city has. What will become of them if Cape Coral grows to 450,000 people? What will become of our official city bird, the Burrowing Owl? Since Cape Coral could have as high as one-third of the state's total population of owls, we must protect them for the future. In the 1800s, hundreds of Burrowing Owls colonies were found in the Lake Kissimmee area in Central Florida. Today, you would be hard-pressed to find one there. Agriculture, farming, as well as housing developments have displaced them.

We cannot let that happen in Cape Coral. As the owls moved from the open central plains of the state to the more congested areas, they met up with automobile collisions, stray domestic animals, pesticides, and human harassment. This quickly led to them being listed as a species of special concern. The Burrowing Owl's status was elevated to threatened as these threats increased state-wide. Land clearing was beneficial for the owls initially, but land clearing led to development and loss of habitat. Statistics show that reproduction rates are not as high in disturbed areas. Education programs, especially in schools, must be given to stress the importance of preserving the Burrowing Owls and why they need protection. These programs must start with the school children, extend to homeowners, and especially target those in the construction industry.

Burrowing Owls are most successful, where it is 50-75% developed, but there will be no more empty lots for the owls to make their homes in the future. Cape Coral is slated for 100% build-out. Parking lots, roads, and lawns will prevent the owls from moving elsewhere. Increased use of pesticides will poison them, and the increased population of humans will bring an increased number of cats roaming the streets and killing the owls. The future doesn't look promising for the poor little owls.

Is there hope for a future for our Official City Bird? Will future generations only see them on YouTube? Can something be done now to allow the owls and humans to co-exist? The most promising solution is to install starter burrows on private properties. Based on the 2009 study done by the city to help develop a long-term plan for these owls, the future lies in these starter burrows. Was this a study that was done and went nowhere? Marco Island, located about an hour south of Cape Coral, has an estimated 500 Burrowing Owls living there. The City Council there signed "an agreement with Audubon and FWCC (Florida Fish and Wildlife Conservation Commission) to pay homeowners for successful starter burrows. The agreement includes a $250 incentive for each year a property owner keeps a potentially occupied starter burrow."

The Future

One only must read the Endangered Species Act of 1973 to understand why we should be proactive rather than reactive when protecting the Burrowing Owl in Cape Coral. While the Burrowing Owls in Cape Coral were listed as a "species of special concern," little attention was paid to them. When they were elevated to a "threatened species," Cape Coral passed ordinances aligned with state laws. Keeping 33 feet away from a burrow during nesting season and when chicks are present are now enforceable ordinances here in the city. Besides being stricter with Burrowing Owls, Cape Coral has a strict Bald Eagle ordinance that is even stricter than what is in place by Florida law.

If the Burrowing Owl is listed as "endangered" in the future, will all building on these empty lots be halted? There are strict laws when an endangered species lives or could live on a piece of land. Can you imagine what would happen in Cape Coral if building permits were not issued if an owl was found on a property or known to have been on the property? Can you imagine the kettle of worms this could open for the city and homeowners? Many people who purchased the land where they planned to retire could no longer build.

Today, most of the people in Cape Coral like the Burrowing Owls. The tide would certainly change against them if, suddenly, lot owners could not build on their lots or builders could no longer find lots to build new homes. Burrowing Owls would fall into disfavor mighty fast. Now is the time to help our City Bird. The citizens of Cape Coral have the chance of helping the long-term survival of the owls. The City of Cape Coral has a set of current and proposed strategies developed (which can be found on the city website) to protect the owls, but how aggressively they are being followed remains to be seen.

CHAPTER 19 Starter Burrows

What is a Starter Burrow????

As was mentioned before, in 2009, a firm was hired by the City of Cape Coral to develop a long-term plan for the Burrowing Owls. At the time, how many owls or burrows existed in the city was unknown. Part of the study was to determine how many burrows there were in the city. A team from the firm and volunteers from Cape Coral Friends of Wildlife canvassed the entire city, counted burrows, and came up with 2700 burrows. From that study, it was concluded that the owls' long-term survival depended on having homeowners put a starter burrow on their front lawns. Cape Coral is projected to grow, so fewer and fewer empty lots will be available for the owls. If the species is to thrive long term, they must have a suitable habitat, so a starter burrow is one solution.

Historically, lawns are not native to the Americas as we know them. Most of the New World was prairie or woodlands, and nowhere were pristine lawns found. Early European settlers found that the grasses that grew here were unsuitable for feeding the livestock they brought to America. They brought seeds from the grass they grew in their homelands, which were not native there either, but the product of deforestation. This new grass grew like wildfire and morphed into our well-manicured lawns.

Florida's "grass" is horrible as it tries to survive the hot Florida sun and long periods of drought mixed with heavy rain periods. Unless you spray your lawn with fertilizers and do an aggressive job of weed control, you will have very tenacious weeds rather than grass. Many environmentally responsible people do not want chemicals on their lawns and are happy to mow their weeds and have a reasonably nice-looking lawn.

The problem with these lawns is that they are nearly impossible to dig through. To dig a hole, you need to lay a shovel roughly flat on the ground and forcefully slide it along the surface to break the vines rather than dig in the usual way. If digging with a shovel is difficult for a human, it is impossible for a Burrowing Owl. So how in the world can a Burrowing Owl dig a burrow on a front lawn if a human has difficulty digging a hole with a shovel? Starter burrows are needed for the owls.

Digging a Starter Burrow

Owners of new homes where owls previously lived, and homes where owls have never lived, are both perfect sites to install a starter burrow. The installation of a starter burrow is the answer and is quite simple.

This involves first removing a two-foot circular section of grass from the lawn with a shovel. Then a small garden shovel and dig a hole about 4 inches in diameter at about a 45-degree angle as far as you can reach (at least 18 inches) and pile the dirt at the back edge of the hole. (See illustrations below). A t-perch can be added, but is not necessary. For more help on installing a starter burrow, you can call:

Cape Coral Friends of Wildlife at 239-980-2593

FIGURE 46 STARTER BURROW CONSTRUCTION

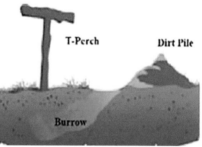

FIGURE 47 HOMEOWNER INSTALLED STARTER BURROWS

Starter burrows can be incorporated into the landscape as this homeowner had done or put in a suitable area on the lawn. The burrow on the left would not be seen if it weren't for the T-perch in the photo. Some residents of Cape Coral that have installed starter burrows on their properties have gone that extra mile to attract a Burrowing Owl, as seen in the following photos. Burrowing Owls have a high tolerance for living near humans. When approached, they will puff up and emit an "eeeeeek sound to warn you to keep away. They will try to look as ferocious as possible and may even swoop over your head. But the city has never received a report of anyone being injured by a Burrowing Owl. So having a Burrowing Owl on your lawn is not dangerous to humans or pets.

Below are some photos of Burrowing Owl sites that property owners have embellished. If these items were installed when the starter burrow was installed, this would be all right, but digging stakes in the ground near an existing burrow is illegal and dangerous because you might collapse the burrow or injure owls inside.

FIGURE 48 HOMEOWNER EMBELLISHMENTS TO BURROWS.

The Susan B. and Anthony photo was taken in front of a bank. I always thought they should name one of the chicks Penny.

CHAPTER 20 The Economics of Wildlife Viewing

I know everyone hates statistics, but these are interesting. Every few years, Florida Fish and Wildlife Commission (FWCC) conducts a study to determine the economic benefit wildlife viewing has on Florida's economics. The 2011 study showed that "wildlife viewing is the second most popular outdoor recreation activity in Florida, surpassing such activities as bicycling, fishing, golf and tennis" and only trailing behind beachgoing as a reason people come to Florida. Certainly, coming to see the Burrowing Owls fall into this category of "wildlife viewing" and add to the state's economy. Just how much wildlife viewing adds to the economy is nothing short of amazing.

Statistics from this study, in part are:

Revenue to the State of Florida is nearly five billion dollars

8.4 million visitors come to Florida for wildlife viewing vs. 3.4 that visit Arizona.

Florida is #1 in the country for total days of wildlife viewing by nonresident visitors

Average age 46-56

The average household income of those visitors is $55-66,000

The most popular away-from-home activities were observing and photographing wildlife.

Florida ranks second in the nation for the number of residents who take trips to view wildlife (1.4 million people)

Of the 1.9 million participants in away-from-home wildlife viewing, photographing, or feeding wildlife, nearly 1.6 million of those did so of birds, and 624,370 took photos of birds of prey, the category Burrowing Owls fall under.

Wildlife viewing supports 44,623 jobs, which is more than the air transportation industry (35,268)

State tax revenue $284,980,784

The $2.7 billion people spend to view wildlife in Florida is more than double the state's annual orange harvest value. Of the $2.7 billion spent on viewing wildlife, $2.3 billion is spent in the Cape Coral /Fort Myers area, the state's highest amount.

People come from all over the world and the U. S. to see the Burrowing Owls of Cape Coral. We have had visitors from South Africa, the Philippines, Germany, the UK, Sweden, Alaska, and around the United States. People get up at ungodly hours of the morning to come to Cape Coral at sunrise to get the best light to photograph these beautiful birds. We have a couple who live in Texas that get on a plane, come to Cape Coral to photograph the owls, go to dinner at a local restaurant, and then take a flight home.

While these people are in town, they eat at the Lobster Lady, Merrick's Seafood, and Annie's Restaurant (after checking out the owls across the street) and stay overnight at the Dolphin Inn, The Weston, Hampton Inn, and local BnB's. They come to town and spend money! The photo below is of a group from Venice, FL, Audubon Society. After hearing a talk about the Burrowing Owls at one of their meetings, thirty-five members drove down to Cape Coral to see them in person.

Figure 49 Audubon Society group touring Cape Coral

According to the statistics from that FWC study, the visitors that come to Florida to observe wildlife are in their late forties and early fifties. For the most part, they are college-educated and have an average income of $66,000. Wouldn't it be in the city's best interest to show these people what a great place Cape Coral would be to retire? Maybe this would even be a win-win situation for the city and the owls. If these people come to see wildlife and the owls, they must care about the environment and be more than willing to help preserve the Burrowing Owls and other wildlife in Cape Coral. They would be happy to put a starter burrow on the front lawn of their new home.

The city is missing the boat when it comes to these owls. Willis Point, Texas, celebrates its Bluebirds, Roscommon, Michigan, its Kirtland's Warbler, La Plata, Maryland, celebrates the Purple Martin; and Atwater, Texas, celebrates its Prairie Chicken. Cape Coral should be doing more to celebrate its Official City Bird. Sure, our Annual Burrowing Owl Festival attracts thousands of people, and our annual Ground Owl Day in February, but this bird should be celebrated all year long. There should be a place where people can go to learn about them. A visitors' center with a continuous loop movie about the owls and throw in a gift shop to help pay the expenses should be the bare minimum. These little visitor centers/gift shops are at many tourist attractions; why cannot we have one here? Cape Coral is planning a massive redevelopment project for its downtown area. Shouldn't a little site be set aside for the Burrowing Owls and our other wildlife? You can read the City's "Current and Proposed Conservation Strategies to Protect Athene cunicularia floridana (Florida Burrowing Owl)" on the city website. You will read and see that the city has written strategies to protect the Burrowing Owl. A visitors' center is a way they can implement one strategy they propose. Many things can be done to both protect the Burrowing Owl and bring revenue into the city. It would be a win-win for both.

JUVENILE BURROWING OWLS

CHAPTER 21 Laws and Ethics

The status of the Burrowing Owl and the laws and ordinances about them have been mentioned throughout this book, but here they are in one simple place to read.

In 2018, when the Burrowing Owl's status changed from a species of special concern to a threatened species, new ordinances were put into place in Cape Coral. These new ordinances mirror those already in place on both the state and federal levels but give local authorities more ability to enforce the existing laws.

Nesting season runs from February 15th through July 14th. City ordinances require that you stay 33 feet away from a burrow during nesting season. During the non-nesting season, you may approach within 10 feet of a burrow, providing there are no chicks in the nest. Occasionally the owls produce young as early as November, so the 33-foot rule would apply, even though it is the non-nesting season.

FIGURE 50 HARASSED BURROWING OWL STANCE

Being able to approach the burrow within 10 feet does not permit you to harass the owls. Harassment means to "harm, pursue, hunt, shoot, wound, kill, trap, capture, or collect, or an attempt to engage in any such conduct." Lying on the ground with a 500 mm lens at the 10-foot mark for an hour would be considered harassment. If you see an owl looking like Figure 50 above, you are TOO CLOSE! Get back and leave the owl alone.

If you are baiting the owl, preventing it from leaving the nest to get food or engaging in behavior that would cause the owl to fly to get a "flight shot," you are also harassing the owl. Cape Coral residents are very protective of "their" owls and will call the authorities. Before the change in the owls' status, it often took quite a while for FWC to respond to harassment issues, but new Cape Coral ordinances allow local authorities such as the Code Compliance Department to be called, so enforcement of the laws is much quicker. In 2018, alert neighbors called the police to report workers from a landscaping company that destroyed six burrows on a construction site. This violation of the ordinance brought them fines, and they even spent some time in jail. Figure 50 was given to me by a photographer, along with some beautiful other photos. I informed him that getting this close to an owl to cause it to take this stance was illegal and to please maintain a safe distance from the owl. He admitted he wasn't aware he was doing anything wrong.

Federal Migratory Bird Treaty Act (In Part)

The Migratory Bird Treaty Act of 1918 (MBTA) is a U.S. federal law intended to protect migratory birds in the United States and Canada. The MBTA makes it illegal for anyone to "take, possess, import, export, transport, sell, purchase, barter, or offer for sale, purchase, or barter any migratory bird, or the parts, nests, or eggs of such a bird except under the terms of a valid permit issued pursuant to Federal regulations.

This federal law makes it illegal to destroy a burrowing owl nest, whether it is occupied or not. So, closing a burrow to sell a property would be a federal offense and could result in a $15,000 fine and 6 months in prison.

ABA Code of Ethics Birding Ethics - American Birding Association

1. Respect and promote birds and their environment.

Support the conservation of birds and their habitats. Engage in and promote bird friendly practices whenever possible, such as keeping cats and other domestic animals indoors or controlled, acting to prevent window strikes, maintaining safe feeding stations, landscaping with native plants, drinking shade-grown coffee, and advocating for conservation policies. Be mindful of any negative environmental affects of your activities, including contributing to climate change. Reduce or offset such affects as much as you are able.

Avoid stressing birds or exposing them to danger. Be particularly cautious around active nests and nesting colonies, roosts, display sites, and feeding sites. Limit the use of recordings and other audio methods of attracting birds, particularly in heavily birded areas, for species that are rare in the area, and for species that are threatened or endangered. Always exercise caution and restraint when photographing, recording, or otherwise approaching birds.

Always minimize habitat disturbance. Consider the benefits of staying on trails, preserving snags, and similar practices.

2. Respect and promote the birding community and its individual members.

Be an exemplary ethical role model by following this Code and leading by example.

Always bird and report with honesty and integrity.

Respect the interests, rights, and skill levels of fellow birders, as well as people participating in other outdoor activities. Freely share your knowledge and experience and be especially helpful to beginning birders.

Share bird observations freely, provided such reporting would not violate other sections of this Code, as birders, ornithologists, and conservationists derive considerable benefit from publicly available bird sightings.

Approach instances of perceived unethical birding behavior with sensitivity and respect; try to resolve the matter in a positive manner, keeping in mind that perspectives vary. Use the situation as an opportunity to teach by example and to introduce more people to this Code.

In group birding situations, promote knowledge by everyone in the group of the practices in this Code and ensure that the group does not unduly interfere with others using the same area.

3. Respect and promote the law and the rights of others.

Never enter private property without the landowner's permission. Respect the interests of and interact positively with people living in the area where you are birding.

Familiarize yourself with and follow all laws, rules, and regulations governing activities at your birding location. In particular, be aware of regulations related to birds, such as disturbance of protected nesting areas or sensitive habitats and the use of audio or food.

Birding should be fun and help build a better future for birds, for birders and for all people.

Birds and birding opportunities are shared resources that should be open and accessible to all.

Birders should always give back more than they take.

CHAPTER 22   Yes, You Can Build

I do not know how many times I have begun a talk about the Burrowing Owls, and the first thing someone says is, "Yea, you can't,"...... and I stop them dead in their tracks because I know what they are going to say. They will say that you can not build a house if a Burrowing Owl exists on the lot. This is just false information. Yes, some specific rules and regulations govern issuing a permit to build, but "YES," you can build.

There is nothing more discouraging than having owned a piece of property in Cape Coral for many years with plans to retire here, only to find a Burrowing Owl living on the lot. Well-meaning people will tell you that you cannot build your dream home with this little bird living here, so what do you do? Most importantly, you shouldn't destroy the nest, even if you think it has been abandoned. That nest is federally protected, and you can get into serious trouble by doing damage to the burrow.

Cape Coral Friends of Wildlife, the wildlife volunteer group in the city, has taken GPS coordinates of every known burrow in Cape Coral. This information is in the city database, so if a permit is pulled on a piece of property, the city knows if a burrow is on the property.

If you plan to build, your first step would be to go to the city website and download the Contractors Information Sheet that gives you all the information you need to get the necessary permits to build. In many cases, with proper protection of the burrow and possibly some home plan modifications, construction can occur any time of the year.

If the burrow is in an area where it cannot be protected, construction must be delayed until after nesting season in July. Then, after all "reasonable alternatives are impractical," a permit to "take" the burrow may be issued by the Executive Director of the Florida Fish and Wildlife Conservation Commission, as well as the U.S. Fish and Wildlife Service. The burrow must be inactive, meaning there will be no flightless young or eggs present in the burrow. The City of Cape Coral has no control over the permitting process and cannot issue permits to destroy (take) a burrow.

You will be directed to the Florida Fish and Wildlife Conservation Commission (FWCC) website with guidelines detailing what is involved in building on a lot where a Burrowing Owl is present. You will find that you can build your dream home with the proper protections in place and perhaps some modifications to your plans.

If you have owned the lot for many years, plan on retiring to Cape Coral, and know you have Burrowing Owl on the lot, plan your building time. Get all your permitting processes taken care of so that building can take place outside of the owl's nesting season.

FWC has options for building on a lot that has a Burrowing Owl burrow on the site and is as follows:

"Three Development Options:

If a Burrowing Owl burrow is present on a vacant lot, one of three scenarios can occur, depending on the proximity of the owl burrow to the proposed development.

Avoid construction on the vacant lot.

During & after construction, maintain a 10-foot buffer zone in all directions from the burrow.

If a 10-foot buffer zone cannot be maintained; a state permit from FWCC to remove an inactive burrow (take).

If the burrow is located within the building envelope, FWC may issue a destroy permit for the owl burrow as a last resort after all reasonable alternatives are exhausted. When a burrow is removed due to new construction, to minimize the adverse impact on the owls when a nest is destroyed, the contractor or homeowners strongly urged to install a starter burrow on the same property. Figure 51 is an active construction site with a Burrowing Owl on the property. A permit was pulled, and a 10-foot perimeter was placed around the burrow. In front of the black fencing is a small red and white sign. On the wooden stake to the right of that sign you can barely see a burrowing owl standing on the top of the stake. This burrow is in an ideal position to be left as is, and hopefully the owls will remain at the site.

FIGURE 51 CORDONED OFF CONSTRUCTION SITE

CHAPTER 23 A Bird in Hand is Worth Everything

FIGURE 52 AUTHOR WITH INJURED OWL

During my years of working with these owls, I had never held one until one day when I received a call from the city asking if I would go out and try to capture an injured Burrowing Owl. All the usual people that did the rescuing in town were unavailable, and since the owl was near my house, they asked if I could help. I agreed. Armed with towels and a fishing net, I went to the address I was given. I quickly located the owl and saw that it indeed had an injured wing. I surveyed the area and saw two burrow entrances with another owl near the entrance to one burrow. I quickly covered the burrow openings to prevent the owl from going back into the burrow. As I approached the injured owl, it ran into the culvert under the driveway. Ok, how am I going to get it out of there? Soon, the man who reported the owl arrived. We came up with an idea. Owls do not like water, so let's try running water into the culvert. The man found a hose and quickly had water running. The aim was not to spray the owl but to just cause a stream of water on the ground. It worked like a charm. As the water approached, the owl kept backing up, right into my waiting net. I quickly and carefully removed the owl from the net and wrapped it in one of the towels I had brought. The owl soon calmed down, and I think deep down, it knew I was trying to help him.

CAPE CORAL BURROWING OWLS DON'T HOOT

The City of Cape Coral has a transport plan for injured wildlife to get them to C.R.O.W., the Clinic for the Rehabilitation of Wildlife on nearby Sanibel Island. The injured animals can be taken to a local veterinarian who arranges to have a volunteer meet a volunteer from C.R.O.W. at the Sanibel Bridge (to avoid us having to pay the bridge toll). The animal is then taken to C.R.O.W. While I waited for the pickup, I could hold a fantastic creature. Those huge lemon-colored eyes peered out of the towel, looking more like E.T. from the movie E.T. The Extraterrestrial than it looked like an owl. I was amazed at how light it was, the weight barely perceptible in my hands. Yet this half-pound creature was capable of flight, deadly accurate hunting, tender care of its young, ingenious adaptations to protect its home and family, and so many other marvelous capabilities. I was truly blessed to have this chance not only to hold a bird in my hands but to hold a Burrowing Owl is something few people have that opportunity. After years of working with the owls, this was a magical moment for me, but a bittersweet one. The owl was injured, and its fate at that moment was unknown. Nevertheless, I held a Burrowing Owl.

***Engaging in any new adventure comes with a learning curve. This photo was taken long before I learned that gloves should always be worn when handling a wild animal. Now I know better!

CHAPTER 24 Fire and Cracker

FIGURE 52 FIRE AND CRACKER

By proclamation of the Mayor of Cape Coral several years ago, the Burrowing Owl is now the official City Bird. While we rarely make it a practice to name the owls in Cape Coral (there are too many!), there are two owls in town by the names of Fire and Cracker.

Now, the two birds, Fire and Cracker, in Figure 52 are unique because where would be a better place for them to live than the Cape Coral Chamber of Commerce? As visitors come into Cape Coral over the lower Cape Coral Bridge, the first building they come to is the Chamber of Commerce. Who knows how many visitors stop by here for information about our city, and these two little ambassadors to the city go virtually unnoticed? People from all over the world come to Cape Coral just to see the Burrowing Owls, and here they are, ten feet from the parking lot. Shouldn't there be a sign telling people that Cape Coral is home to the World's Largest Population of the Florida subspecies of this beautiful little threatened bird? How many towns do you visit and see a huge sign proclaiming the football team won some state award 15 years ago, and the sign is still up? Don't these owls deserve some kind of sign???? Don't they deserve some recognition?

95

CAPE CORAL BURROWING OWLS DON'T HOOT

Wait! The story gets better. They are named Fire and Cracker because every July 4th; the city shoots off fireworks from the Cape Coral Bridge. Someone decided that the owls should be moved to another park because someone might trip in the burrow and possibly hurt their ankle during the celebration. Flashback! Remember reading that all burrows are marked with PVC pipes. The park they live in is just a manicured area under a bridge and is mainly used by anglers. The park they were to be moved to is used by joggers, dog walkers, children's festivals, and garden club festivals and is a bustling park full of trees. Not the place a Burrowing Owl would choose to live.

Relocation of a Burrowing Owl is not as simple as just moving them from place to place. Out west, when they relocate Burrowing Owls, they are placed in tents for a month to reprogram them and to acclimate them to a new home. If you just move them, they will probably return to their original nest site faster than you could return to the site by car.

Cape Coral Friends of Wildlife offered to set up a perimeter around the owls to protect the burrow during the fireworks. After much back-and-forth deliberation, the owls were finally allowed to stay at the park where they remain.

As a side note, the female owl, Cracker, was perhaps the most unusual bird in the world. She has the extremely rare occurrence of one dark eye and one yellow eye, as seen in Figure 52. As was discussed in the chapter nine, "The Eyes", this is a genetic abnormality that produces some very interesting-looking owls.

CHAPTER 25 Close Encounters of The First Kind

FIGURE 54 HOOVER AND THE BURROWING OWL

My neighbor Bob is an advocate of sorts of "my owls", but this was not always the case. When Bob moved in next door, he came over, and we met on my front lawn. We introduced ourselves and learned we were both from New Jersey, so we had lots to discuss. During the conversation, Bob told us his nickname was "Bob Outdoors," and anything that moves, he shoots, and anything that swims, he catches. All the while, he was scoping out the two little Burrowing Owls that lived on my lawn and were standing by the burrow, watching us.

Oh great, a hunter is living next to me! Now Bob is well over six feet tall and very well built. I, at 5 foot 3 inches, gathered my courage, walked up close to him, and pointed my finger at him. I proceeded to tell him that those birds he has been eyeing over there on my front lawn are protected by the Federal Government, protected by the State of Florida, the City of Cape Coral, and especially protected by Beverly (me), and he had best better leave them alone. I laughed a little so as not to make him angry at me the first time we met, but he knew I was serious.

Well, Bob and I have become good friends, and he has taken a liking to my owls and keeps tabs on them now. He often calls me to report on something the owls did.

One morning Bob calls me at an ungodly hour of the morning (he and I are "early birds "so he knows I am awake) to tell me about an incredible close encounter between his dog, Hoover, and "my" owl. Bob has two retriever dogs, weighing about 100 pounds each. As I have mentioned before, owls gather animal feces and bring it to the burrow. So, as you can imagine, Bob's backyard is an excellent place for the owls to find feces without having to carry it too far.

Around 3 am, Bob let Hoover out in the backyard to do his business, and my owl was out there collecting his dog's poop. Bob spots both Hoover and the owl face to face, a 100-pound dog and a 7-ounce owl, just staring at each other for the longest time. They were both looking at each other, curious as to just what each one was. Can you just imagine the dialog going on between them?

Hoover: "What are you doing in my yard?"

Owl: "I hope you don't mind, but I just came for some poop."

Hoover: "What the heck are you going to do with it?

Owl: "Oh, the wife is sitting on eggs, so I use it to catch dinner. You don't need it, do you?"

Hoover: "Dinner? You don't eat it. Do you???"

Owl.: "NO! It attracts bugs that the wife likes. I catch them and take them to her since she doesn't get out much. It makes me a macho man around the house." When the kids are born, I need to feed her and the kids. Later we use the poop to teach the kids to hunt." Hoover: "How does that work"?

Owl: "Well, we put the poop near our burrow. The poop attracts bugs, and the kids can practice catching the bugs. This way, they are near the house, and if that nasty hawk that likes to sit in the tree in your front yard comes around, we can get them back in the burrow quickly."

Hoover: "That's cool. All this poop does is get us in trouble with Bob. He gets mad when we leave it all over the place, so take all you want; there is a constant supply here." Owl: "Gee, thanks; Heaven knows I need a constant supply."

Bob was amazed to see this tiny little owl and his huge dog looking at each other and how long it lasted with no negative interaction. Isn't nature amazing?

CHAPTER 26 Books About Owls

"Hoot" by Carl Hiaasen

The most famous book about the Burrowing Owls of Cape Coral is "Hoot" by Carl Hiaasen, a New York Times bestselling author and columnist for Florida's Miami Herald (now retired) newspaper. Carl has written over 20 novels that can be considered humorous crime stories. Carl's books are interesting, to say the least. Tourist Season, Skinny Dip, Flush, and Scat are among his more well-known books. The underpinnings of all Carl's books are Florida's problems, be it politics, the sugar industry, the python problem in the Everglades, or the tourists. Hiaasen's books are classified as humorous, fiction, and crime-related, and the genre is geared toward an adult audience. When he realized his young nieces and nephews couldn't read his books, he wrote "Hoot," a book geared towards teenagers trying to deal with the problem of Burrowing Owls losing their habitat to construction.

This book is about the antics of three teenagers trying to save some Burrowing Owls from having their burrows destroyed when Mother Paula's Pancake House was scheduled to be built on the property where the owls lived. The property is guarded by a security guard who takes the full brunt of the kid's efforts to stop the construction. The book is written with Cape Coral and its problems with humans, construction, and the owls in mind. It is an excellent book for teenagers, as it shows how just a few people can make a change, especially when it comes to the environment. The book was later made into a movie by the same name and starred Jimmy Buffett. Several Cape Coral Friends of Wildlife members were involved in the film's production. They had bit parts in the movie's filming, but their roles were edited out in the end. Only CCFW member Carl Veaux remains in the crowd scene at the end of the movie. The book has been widely read by teenagers all over the country and has won several literary awards.

Hiaasen donated the original manuscript of "Hoot" to Cape Coral Friends of Wildlife to raise money for the owls. CCFW decided it was best to put the manuscript in the Cape Coral Historical Museum, where it remains today.

The book and the DVD make an excellent gift for teenagers, and both can be purchased on Amazon.

"Buffy the Burrowing Owl"

Betty Gilbert, a longtime resident and photographer from Cape Coral, wrote this book. Geared toward the younger child, telling the story of a young

Burrowing Owl. This book introduces the younger child to the Burrowing Owls and the beauty of wildlife.

Ollie Finds a New Home: The Story of a Burrowing Owl in Cape Coral

This book deals with the ever-increasing problem of the Burrowing Owls of Cape Coral needing to find a new home when development forces them out of their existing homes. This book was written by Roseanne Pawelec (Author) and illustrated by Sue Lynn Cotton.

Other books about Burrowing Owls

World of Burrowing Owls: A Photographic Essay Exploring

Their Behaviors & Beauty by Rob Palmer, Rob Palmer

Burrowing Owls by Melissa Hill

My Little Book of Burrowing Owls (Part of the My Little Book Series) by Hope Irvin

Marston

Florida Burrowing Owls by Betty Gilbert

Owls! Fun Facts for Kids by Donna Trueman, B. Ed

Facts about the burrowing owl, A Picture Book for Kids, by Lisa Strattin

Birds of Prey, Eagles, Ospreys, Hawks, Burrowing Owls and Crested Caracaras by Norman Wei

CAPE CORAL BURROWING OWLS DON'T HOOT

Animal Knowledge, burrowing Owl, by Catherine L. Hayes

Reggie, the Burrowing Owl, by Derrick Wood and Thomas Wood

How Burrowing Owls Lead to Vomiting Anarchists by Kelsey Westphal and Kim-

Mai Cutler

Coloring Book Reggie the burrowing Owl: The True Story of

How a Family Found and Raised a burrowing owl by Thomas J.

Wood and Derrick Woodlive

CHAPTER 27   Burrowing Owls Around the World

In December 2022, I visited Peru on a vacation/birding trip. One of my prime goals for the trip besides seeing Machu Picchu was to see the Burrowing Owls of Peru. In researching the Internet, I saw a brochure for a tour company that pictured a Burrowing Owl on their cover. I contacted the company and asked about the possibility of seeing a Burrowing Owl. They told me I had a 90% chance of seeing one, so I booked a private tour with them. On the day of the tour, they told me they would pick me up at 5:30 am. Since the hotel I was staying at was on a narrow cobblestone street, they could not drive the van up to the hotel, but the guide would pick me up. On time, the guide arrived at the hotel. I figured the transportation would be a block away, but it wasn't. He thankfully took my backpack, and off we went semi-jogging through the streets of Lima. Fortunately, I am an early bird, so this early arising was not a problem, but I am also not a spring chicken, so keeping up with this young, fit guide was a challenge. Adding to this fact, most of the streets of Peru are paved with stones of all different sizes, so walking and running is even more challenging. Thankfully, I purchased a walking stick at Machu Picchu, which made the little jaunt a bit easier.

We finally made it to the van where the driver was waiting for us, and off we went for a 65-mile (100km) trip to the Lachay National Reserve.

Interestingly, even though Lima, Peru is in the sub-tropics, 10% of it is a desert. Lima (home to half of all the Peruvians) is the second largest city in the world that is built in a desert; only Cairo in Egypt is larger. The only moisture the area receives is from fog from the ocean and occasional drizzling rain. When you picture a desert, you visualize the hot blazing sun, but in the Peruvian desert, the thick fog keeps the sun from shining through, and the landscape is rather gray. The weather is divided into rainy and dry seasons, and the seasons are reversed from ours. The colder months, aka winter, are from June through October, and the rainy season is from December through April. May and November are the months that the weather can swing either way. By taking this trip on December 1st, I should have been in the rainy season, but the weather held out, and I had genuinely nice weather.

After the 2.5-hour ride, we arrived at Lachay National Reserve in the Atacama Desert. Since the area was coming out of the dry season, vegetation was very sparse, and it looked like the Western U.S. prairies. (Check out the backgrounds in Figures 55 and 56.) The first thing we were greeted with after the entrance sign was a sign that said: "Horario de Atencion" (Hours of Operation) and a picture of a Burrowing Owl on it. Peru has recorded over 1800 species of birds, and they picked the photogenic Burrowing Owl to put on the sign. Too cool!

FIGURE 55 LACHAY NATIONAL RESERVE

There are over 20 subspecies of Burrowing Owls in the Americas. North America has 2 sub-species, the Western Burrowing Owl and Florida Burrowing Owl. Peru, being the 19th largest country in the world with a coastline of 1500 miles (2,414km), is home to four sub-species of Burrowing Owls.

FIGURE 56 WELCOME SIGN TO LACHAY

Below is a chart showing the four sub-species in Peru, their taxonomic name, and their range.

CAPE CORAL BURROWING OWLS DON'T HOOT

Southwest Peruvian Burrowing Owl (Athene cunicularia nanotes) Found in the southwestern area of Peru along with the Intermediate Burrowing Owl

West Peruvian Burrowing Owl (Athene cunicularia intermedia)   Found in Southwestern Peru

Junin Burrowing Owl or South Andean Burrowing Owl (Athene cunicularia juninesis)   Found in Central Peru northward through Bolivia and into Argentina

Puna Island Burrowing Owl (Athene cunicularia punensis) Found in the extreme northern Peru into Ecuador

Lima is in the north-central area of Peru, so the Junin Burrowing Owl (Athene cunicularia juninesis) would be found there.

In Spanish, one name for the Burrowing Owls is Lechuza Terrestre. The word Lechuza means owl in Spanish, so I wonder if Lachay National Preserve was actually named after the Burrowing Owl. If it was, that would be rather amazing, given all the birds in Peru.

We drove down a dusty road, and it was not long before my guide spotted a pair of Burrowing Owls not far off the road. I could see no outward difference in the appearance between the Peruvian owls and the Florida owls. There must be some difference as they are considered different sub-species. I noted that they did have much bigger burrows. The entrances appeared to be nearly a foot in diameter as opposed to the burrows dug here in Florida, which are only 4-6 inches wide. After riding through the preserve and spotting several more Burrowing Owls, we drove to "the other side of the mountain", still within the reserve. This habitat was much different, in that it had a lot of cacti and was very rocky. There were also owls, and I doubt they were digging a burrow there. Unfortunately, my camera died, and I didn't get photos of this side of the mountain.

Scientists studying the ecosystem of these arid deserts find that owls contribute to the appearance of plant life. As the owls dig their burrows, the dry crusty soil is disturbed, and seeds can become buried. This allows moisture to accumulate and allows the seeds to germinate. So, the Burrowing Owls are indeed important to the desert ecosystem.

FIGURE 57 PERUVIAN BURROWING OWLS

Following is what Burrowing Owls are called in other countries.

Graveugle (Norwegian)

Pójdzka Ziemna (Polish)

Coruja-buraqueira (Portuguese)

Mochuelo de Madriguera (Spanish)

Prärieuggla (Swedish)

Buf I varrosur (Albanian)

Berogh bu (Armenian) Buina sova (Bulgarian)

Buri sova (Croatian)

Gravende uil (Dutch)

Eule graben (German)

'O Burrows Owl (Hawaiian)

Tylluan uwn (Welsh)

Ulchabhán tochailte (Irish)

CAPE CORAL BURROWING OWLS DON'T HOOT

Gravende ugle (Danish)

Grawe uil (Afrikaans)

Lulu ena siko (Fijian)

Gufo scavatorio (Italian)

Pag-aalab ng utang (Filipino)

CHAPTER 28 Taxonomy

Thanks to our sandy soil and wide-open spaces, the Burrowing Owls in Cape Coral, Florida, have flourished, making this the epicenter of the Athene cunicularia floridana, better known as the Florida Burrowing Owl. For those with a scientific side, the taxonomy of the Burrowing Owl is as follows:

Order: Strigiformes (all owls belong to this order)

Family: Strigoides (all owls belong to this family except barn owls)

Genus: Athene (the name derived from Athene, the goddess of night, the goddess of war, wisdom, and the liberal arts.)

Species: Athene cunicularia (Burrowing Owl)

Sub-species: floridana

The official scientific name for our Burrowing Owls in Florida is Athene cunicularia floridana; quite a mouthful for a little bird!

According to the Handbook of the Birds of the World, under the genus Athene, there are five owls listed:

- The Burrowing Owl (Athene cunicularia), found in the United States and the Caribbean
- Spotted Owlet (Athene brama), found in Asia
- Forest Spotted Owlet (Athene blewitti)
- Little Owl (Athene noctua) is in Europe, Asia, and North Africa.
- White-browed Owl (Athene superciliaris) An owl recently found in Madagascar added to this genus.

Of these owls, the Forest Spotted Owl is Critically Endangered. Previously thought to be extinct, it was re-discovered in central India.

FIGURE 58 LITTLE OWL

According to Wikipedia, there are 18 recognized sub-species of Burrowing Owls, two of which are extinct. The 18 recognized subspecies are:

†A. c. amaura (Lawrence, 1878): Antiguan burrowing owl – formerly Antigua, Saint Kitts, and Nevis Islands, extinct (circa 1905)

A. c. boliviana (L. Kelso, 1939): Bolivian burrowing owl – the Bolivian altiplano

A. c. brachyptera (Richmond, 1896): Margarita Island burrowing owl – Margarita Island, might include A. c.apurensis

A. c. carrikeri (Stone, 1922): east Colombian burrowing owl – eastern Colombia, doubtfully distinct from A. c. tolimae

A. c. cunicularia (Molina, 1782):- southern burrowing owl – lowlands of southern Bolivia and southern Brazil south to Tierra del Fuego

A. c. floridana (Ridgway, 1874): Florida burrowing owl – Florida and the Bahamas; listed as Vulnerable[11]

A. c. grallaria (Temminck, 1822): Brazilian burrowing owl – central and eastern Brazil

†A. c. guadeloupensis (Ridgway, 1874): Guadeloupe burrowing owl – formerly Guadeloupe and Marie-Galante Islands, extinct (circa 1890)

A. c. guantanamensis (Garrido, 2001): Cuban burrowing owl – Cuba and Isla de la Juventud

108

A. c. hypugaea (Bonaparte, 1825): western burrowing owl – southern Canada through the Great Plains south to Central America; listed as Apparently Secure[12]

A. c. juninensis (Berlepsch & Stolzmann, 1902): south Andean burrowing owl – Andes from central Peru to northwestern Argentina, might include A. c. punensis.

A. c. minor (Cory, 1918): Guyanese burrowing owl – southern Guyana and Roraima region

A. c. nanodes (Berlepsch & Stolzmann, 1892): southwest Peruvian burrowing owl – southwestern Peru, might include A. c. intermedia

A. c. pichinchae (Boetticher, 1929): west Ecuadorean burrowing owl – western Ecuador

A. c. rostrata (C. H. Townsend, 1890): Revillagigedo burrowing owl – Clarion Island, Revillagigedo Islands

A. c. tolimae (Stone, 1899): west Colombian burrowing owl – western Colombia, might include A. c. carrikeri

A. c. troglodytes (Wetmore & Swales, 1931): Hispaniolan burrowing owl – Hispaniola (Haiti and the Dominican Republic) and surrounding islands (Gonâve Island, Beata Island)

CHAPTER 29 Driving in Cape Coral

Wanna have some fun???? Cape Coral is the 5th largest city, land-wise, in Florida. It covers over 100 square miles and is intersected by 400 miles of canals. Most of the streets end in dead ends, and few roads traverse the entire peninsula, so finding your way around town can be daunting. Modern GPS has come a long way and is helpful for not getting lost, but you can quickly get yourself turned around.

Knowing the grid system of Cape Coral helps steer you in the right direction, but it is rumored that the designers of the roadway system were slightly under the influence of spirits when laying out the city grid. This rumor has never been substantiated. So here goes an explanation of the system. After reading this, you will probably be totally confused, so either upgrade your rental to a car with GPS or make sure you have a phone with GPS capability. You won't regret it!

Santa Barbara Boulevard, the centerline on the map above, runs in a north-south direction nearly the entire length of the city. After it crosses Pine Island

Road (CR 78), the name changes to Juanita Boulevard. This road divides Cape Coral in half, east to west. The north and south divisions are not as clearly defined as the east-west ones. Embers Parkway divides the city into north and south quadrants west of Santa Barbara Boulevard. East of Santa Barbara Boulevard, Hancock Bridge Parkway divides the city into the north and south.

Most roads are numbered and originate from the center of that cross in the middle of the map and get larger as they spread out. At or near the junction of Santa Barbara Boulevard, Embers Parkway, and Hancock Bridge Parkway, you can find roads named NW 3rd Avenue, SW 3rd Avenue, NE 3rd Avenue, and SE 3rd Avenue. All road numbers start at this point and go east, west, north, or south. All road names begin with the building's number, then the quadrant where they originate, followed by the street number and then a designated ending for lack of a better word (for example, 2549 SW 3rd Avenue). In the scheme of things, the A's, B's, C's, and P's run north and south while the S's, T's, and L's run east and west. So that means that Avenues, Boulevards, Courts, and Places run north and south while Streets, Terraces, and Lanes run east and west. Parkways such as Cape Coral Parkway, Embers Parkway, Veterans Parkway, etc., are major east-west roads. The major north-south roads are boulevards such as Del Prado Boulevard, Santa Barbara Boulevard, and Chiquita Boulevard.

Now that you are thoroughly confused, it is simple to remember that if you are traveling north or south, the street numbers go up from that center point and alternate between streets and terraces with an occasional lane thrown in. If you are traveling east on SE 10th Street, you will have to go at least 20 blocks before reaching SE 20th Street. You will pass SE 11th Street, SE 11th Terrace, SE 12th Street, SE 12th Terrace, and so on, with an occasional lane thrown in. Going north and south, Avenues and Places and Courts alternate, with an occasional boulevard thrown in.

If you are looking for a particular address, note which quadrant it is in—NE, SE, NW, SW), whether it is on an avenue, boulevard, court, place (n-s roadway), or a street, terrace, lane, or parkway (e-w roadway), and you need the house or building number. Remember, they also spread out from the center point, so the lower the number, the closer to the central crossroads.

Oh, I almost forgot. If the road is "S" curved like Coronado Parkway shown in the map below, the road still follows the same convention. From Cape Coral Parkway, Coronado Parkway goes in a northern direction for a short distance, then becomes an east-west road, and the numbers get smaller. In the beginning, it follows the north-south numbering system as it heads north. As it curves to the right, it begins its east-west numbering. So, you will pass SE 46th Lane, then SE 46th Terrace; as the road curves, the next street is SE 8th Place, then SE 9th Place. As you continue, you pass Vincennes Blvd (n-s road), then the road curves again, and you are on SE 44th Street. This goes for any other curved road in town, which fortunately is few and far between.

The streets are named near the yacht club and a city park. In some instances, they are named alphabetically, but not always.

If you decide to wander around town yourself, be sure to have a GPS or at least a map and mark your starting location as a waypoint in your GPS or mark a local restaurant or hotel.

In the map below, trace your finger along Coronado Parkway and see how the road names change to fit the numbering sequence of our grid system.

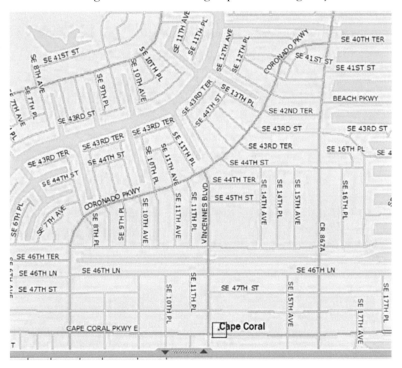

CHAPTER 30 Hotels and Motels in Cape Coral

My husband likes kidney stew, and I do not like being in the same room with this popular English dish. The same goes for hotels. What I may think is a great hotel may be a dive for some people and too expensive for others. With that said, I am listing only the notable hotels in Cape Coral. I would suggest going to TripAdvisor and checking them out by reading the reviews. In addition, in 2022, Hurricane Ian devastated Southwest Florida. The eye passed over Cape Coral, Fort Myers, and Sanibel, laying a path of incredible destruction. Many homes and businesses were wiped off the face of the earth, and some of the hard-hit areas will need to take years to recover. You will need to check to see if the hotel or motel you are interested in is still in business.

The Weston Cape Coral Resort at Marina Village

5951 Silver King Blvd., Cape Coral, FL This is the most expensive hotel in town, with rates off-season at over $100 a night and in-season rates in the $300-600 a night range. The hotel is on the river and features restaurants, a pool, and many other upscale amenities.

Hampton Inn and Suites

619 SE 47th Terrace, Cape Coral, FL This hotel is a relatively new, clean, and nicely appointed hotel. Rates are in the $100 + a night range, depending on the season. The big drawback is the location. It is located across from a hardware store and nothing much else. The plus is that there are Burrowing Owl locations within a short walking distance of this hotel.

Holiday Inn Express,

538 Cape Coral Parkway East, Cape Coral. This hotel is located just over the Cape Coral Bridge, in what is considered "downtown" Cape Coral. Again, these prices are in the $100 range in season. There are restaurants within walking distance, and you have easy access to other attractions in the area. The hotel receives rather helpful reviews, but I hear it can get noisy from the local bar and road traffic.

Hideaway Waterfront Resort,

4601 SE 5th Avenue, Cape Coral. This motel is one of the budget hotels in town. It has been around a while and has gone through some renovations over the years. The place is clean and gets complimentary reviews for the price.

Dolphin Key Resort,

502 Miramar Street, Cape Coral. A reasonably priced motel located closest to our beach situated on the river. It has been in business for a long time; it has gone through major renovations and gets complimentary reviews.

One of Cape Coral's unique features is that it is comprised primarily of single-family residential homes. Looking on sites like Trivago, you can find many of these homes listed for short-term vacation rentals. You can rent a 3-bedroom house for a little more than a hotel room. If you are coming down with family members, this is an idea. Plus, most of these homes are on canals, so you can even fish right in your backyard.

As you can see, there are not many hotels and motels directly in Cape Coral, but just outside the city, within 10 to 45 minutes, there are plenty of places to stay. Cape Coral is only 20 to 25 minutes from Sanibel/Captiva Islands and Fort Myers Beach beaches, 40 minutes from Bonita Springs, and 45 minutes from Naples, depending on traffic. Up and down the western coast of Florida, you will find beaches, fishing, and sun, so hotels and motels are plentiful.

You can find a nice assortment of hotels near the Southwest Florida International Airport at reasonable prices. The closer you get to the beaches, the higher the room rates. If you like the beach scene, t-shirt shops, and plenty of nightlife, Fort Myers Beach used to be an excellent place to stay, but traffic on and off the island was horrendous during the high season and it was devastated by hurricane Ian. There is some good shorebird viewing along the Gulf of Mexico side of the island.

Sanibel and neighboring Captiva Islands are beautiful barrier islands that lie off the coast of Florida on the Gulf of Mexico and are a must-visit stop for bird watchers. I do not know how much damage they sustained, but reports say it was severe, so again, check before you go. Ding Darling National Wildlife Refuge (CLOSED ON FRIDAY'S), Bailey Tract, and the Sanibel lighthouse are beautiful places to see the beautiful Roseate Spoonbills, White Pelicans, herons of all kinds, plovers, sandpipers, migrating hawks, and a plethora of other birds. But again, traffic is horrendous on the island during tourist season, and crossing the bridge is a $6.00 toll. Home prices on Sanibel/Captiva Islands range from $800,000 for a one-bedroom bungalow to over four million dollars for a McMansion. Hotel/motel rates follow similar high prices, but you want to take a trip over there (AT LOW TIDE and NOT ON FRIDAY) during your visit to Southwest Florida. Finding a room during the high season (Jan-Feb-March) can be challenging. BOOK EARLY! AND CHECK FIRST!

CHAPTER 31 You Can Help

Cape Coral Friends of Wildlife

 Cape Coral Friends of Wildlife is a 501 (c)(3) non-profit organization with over 500 members that have made great strides in saving the Burrowing Owls, the Gopher Tortoises, Butterflies, Purple Martins, Manatees, and other wildlife in Cape Coral. Some of the programs and projects they are involved in are:

Community Outreach Programs in the schools and service organizations

Construction of the Tom Allen Butterfly House

Installation of Purple Martin homes around the city and schools for homeschoolers.

Support of The Manatee Cape Connection and Sirenia Vista Park

Annual Ground Owl Day

Sunset Celebration

Annual Burrowing Owl Festival

The Nature of Cape Coral Bus Tours

Protection of Owl and Gopher Tortoise Burrows during Utilities Expansion Project

Marking and taking GPS coordinates of all known burrows in the city

Donate or join by calling Cape Coral Friends of Wildlife at 239-980-2593

Cape Coral Wildlife Trust

In 2017, the Cape Coral Wildlife Trust, a 501(c)(3), was created to acquire lots that have Gopher Tortoises or Burrowing Owls living on them. In the first four years of their existence, the organization acquired fifty lots with active Burrowing Owl burrows or Gopher Tortoise burrows on them.

Cape Coral Wildlife Trust's goal is to create mini environmental parks throughout the city that will be used to educate both locals and visitors about the importance of protecting these species as Cape Coral grows.

CCWT is asking landowners to donate parcels of land that are home to these protected species or to donate parcels that perhaps have been inherited and, over the years, have become a home for these threatened species.

With the cost of land so high, CCWT needs both monetary donations and donations of land, which are greatly appreciated.

In addition to purchasing land, CCWT is promoting the installation of starter burrows on the front lawns of private homes. Burrowing Owls do not require large parcels of land to survive. A front lawn is a suitable habitat, and the installation of starter burrows is a scientifically studied solution to the long-term survival of these owls.

Call 239-980-2593 for more information.

Donate to GO FUND ME

APPENDIX

Cape Coral City ORDINANCE 82 – 18

The following is the ordinance passed by the City Council giving added protection to the Burrowing Owls. These rules mirror those set forth by the State of Florida.

AN ORDINANCE AMENDING THE CITY OF CAPE CORAL CODE OF ORDINANCES, CHAPTER 23, "PROTECTED SPECIES", BY CREATING ARTICLE II, "BURROWING OWL PROTECTION", PROVIDING FOR PURPOSE AND INTENT; PROVIDING FOR DEFINITIONS; PROVIDING FOR DEVELOPMENT STANDARDS; PROVIDING FOR PROTECTION AND

PERMIT PROCEDURES; PROVIDING FOR EXEMPT ACTIVITIES WITHIN

PROTECTION ZONES; PROVIDING FOR PENALTIES; PROVIDING FOR SUPPLEMENTAL REGULATIONS; PROVIDING SEVERABILITY AND AN EFFECTIVE DATE.

WHEREAS, pursuant to Article VIII, Section 2, Constitution of the state of Florida, and Chapter 166, Florida Statutes, the Cape Coral City Council ("Council") is authorized to adopt ordinances, except as otherwise provided by law; and

WHEREAS, the Florida Fish and Wildlife Conservation Commission had previously designated the burrowing owl as a "Species of Special Concern," however, in January 2017, the Commission designated the burrowing owl as a "Threatened Species" in the state of Florida; and

WHEREAS the Council hereby finds that the protection of the burrowing owl is an important public purpose; and

WHEREAS, the Council hereby finds that this ordinance is in the best interest of the public health, safety, and welfare.

NOW, THEREFORE, THE CITY OF CAPE CORAL, FLORIDA, HEREBY ORDAINS THIS ORDINANCE AS FOLLOWS:

SECTION 1. The City of Cape Coral Code of Ordinances, Chapter 23, Article II, is hereby created to read as follows:

ARTICLE II: - BURROWING OWL PROTECTION

§ 23-10 Purpose and intent.

The purpose of this article is to protect and preserve the burrowing owl (Athene cunicularia floridana) by protecting, enhancing, and preserving the burrows of the burrowing owl and its immediate environs. The burrowing owl is currently classified as State Threatened by the Florida Fish and Wildlife Conservation Commission (hereinafter "Commission"). With reasonable and proper management, the population of the burrowing owl can be conserved and improved.

§ 23-11 Definitions.

For this article, the following definitions shall apply unless the context clearly indicates or requires a different meaning:

Active burrow means a potentially occupied burrow that contains eggs or is used by flightless young. (Per Commission guidelines, the Commission typically does not issue permits to take active nests, except in situations involving health and human safety. Removing an active nest may also require a Federal permit from the U.S. Fish and Wildlife Service.)

Applicant means the property owner, or the property owner's agent or authorized representative.

Burrow means a hole or tunnel dug by a small animal to use as a dwelling.

Development means any improvement or change of the land induced by human activities.

Inactive burrow means a potentially occupied burrow that does not contain eggs or flightless young. (Per Commission guidelines, inactive burrows provide important shelter for burrowing owls yearround, and affects to potentially occupied burrows may cause a take, even when burrows are inactive.)

Potentially occupied burrow means a burrow with obvious indications of use and those with minimal or no obvious indications of use. Obvious indicators of use include burrowing owls present in or near the burrow entrance or evidence around the entrance, such as whitewash, feces, pellets, prey remains, or adornments.

Protection zone means the land area that surrounds a burrow.

Take means to harass, harm, pursue, hunt, shoot, wound, kill, trap, capture, or collect, or an attempt to engage in any such conduct. The term "harm" in the definition of take means an act which actually kills or injures a burrowing owl. Such act may include significant habitat modification or degradation where it actually kills or injures burrowing owls by significantly impairing essential behavioral patterns, including breeding, feeding, or sheltering. The term "harass" in the definition of take means an intentional or negligent act or omission which creates the likelihood of injury to a burrowing owl by annoying it to such an extent as to significantly disrupt normal behavioral patterns which include, but are not limited to, breeding, feeding, or sheltering.

§ 23-12 Development standards.

For development, the following, as applicable, shall serve as guidelines or standards for the protection of burrowing owls as prescribed by the goals, objectives, and policies of the conservation and coastal management element of the Cape Coral Comprehensive Plan:

Prior to submission of development applications, the following procedures are required:

Applicants shall conduct a visual survey of the affected property for burrowing owl burrows. If a burrow is found on the subject property or observed on an adjoining property where the protection zone extends into the subject property, the applicant shall contact the Commission for management guidelines. The applicant shall include the visual survey results with the development application and expressly indicate whether a take permit is being sought from the Commission.

In addition to the visual survey required in subsection (a)1., development applications requiring PDP or site plan approval are required to submit an environmental survey of the development site. The environmental survey shall indicate whether there is the presence of burrowing owls or burrows on site; whether the development proposal will affect owl burrows; and whether a take permit is being sought from the Commission.

All development applications will be reviewed against the city database for burrowing owls. If the City database or the surveys required by subsections (a) one. or (a) 2. above indicate the presence of burrowing owls or burrows, the applicant shall submit an affidavit identifying such presence and indicate whether a take permit is being sought from the Commission.

§ 23-13 Protection and permit procedures.

The requirements for taking or protecting the burrowing owl are as follows:

It shall be a violation of this article to take any active or inactive burrowing owl burrow without proper state permits issued by the Commission.

Permits issued by the Commission shall be posted on site during all phases of the construction.

Protection zone requirements shall include the following:

A protection zone having at least a 10-foot buffer during the nonbreeding season (July 11 - February 14), and at least a 33-foot buffer during the breeding season (February 15 July 10), shall be maintained around the entrance of potentially occupied burrows during all phases of construction. A protection 2 @ § 23-14 zone shall comply with Commission guidelines, as such guidelines may be amended.

Contractors and property owners shall be responsible for maintaining the protection zone and informing all employees, workers, agents, and subcontractors to avoid the protection zone and to do nothing to affect the burrow(s) in such a manner as to make it collapse or to cause a take. Contractors and property owners shall be fully responsible for the actions of their employees, workers, agents, and subcontractors to ensure that all applicable laws, rules, and regulations protecting the burrowing owl are adhered to. Any take or violation of this article may subject the contractor and property owner to penalties as provided herein.

The City Building Official, code enforcement officers, law enforcement officers, or other City officials as may be designated by the City Council, may issue stop work orders for any development or construction that is not in compliance with the provisions of this article until any such violations have been inspected and complied with, and until any avoidance, minimization, or mitigation measures required by the Commission have been complied with or satisfied.

All Commission rules and guidelines relating to protection and taking procedures shall be followed at all times, even if not described in this article.

§ 23-14 Exempt activities within protection zones.

The following activities conducted within the protection zone of burrowing owl burrows shall not constitute a violation of this article, with the understanding that if any burrow does collapse or get damaged by the activity, it shall be immediately reported to the Commission and the City of Cape Coral to ensure proper rescue efforts may take place:

CAPE CORAL BURROWING OWLS DON'T HOOT

Burrow maintenance activities for the protection of owls, including the clipping of vegetation within the protection zone, staking, and posting the protection zone with flagging tape and signage, and recording pertinent data.

Contractors and the property owner(s) may enter the protection zone for the limited purpose of removing debris with the full understanding that they can do nothing to disturb or harm the burrowing owl or burrow in any manner. Contractors and lawn maintenance companies shall be fully responsible for the actions of their employees to ensure that all applicable laws, rules, and regulations protecting the burrowing owl are adhered to.

City employees, City agents and representatives, and the property owner(s) may enter the protection zone for the purpose of maintaining vegetation if using equipment that does not exert pressure on the ground to ensure the burrow does not collapse.

Scientific research or investigations approved by the Commission or the United States Fish and Wildlife Service. The City of Cape Coral shall be notified of all such research or investigations and provided with all study reports and publications produced.

Professional environmental consultants that are conducting surveys or monitoring of burrowing owls in conjunction with private or public construction.

§ 23-15 Penalties.

Any person found violating any of the provisions of this article shall, upon conviction, be punished by a fine not to exceed $500 or by imprisonment in the county jail for a period not to exceed 60 days, or by both fine and imprisonment. Such person shall also pay all costs and expenses incurred by the City in instituting such action. Each day a violation continues shall be considered a separate and distinct offense.

In addition to any other penalty provided by this article, any person who violates this article may be required to restore the protection zone to its condition prior to the violation. In the event restoration is not completed within a reasonable time after notice to the violator of the restoration requirement, then the City may perform the restoration and the cost of the restoration shall constitute a lien upon the subject property until paid in full. Any such restoration must be approved by the Commission.

In addition to any other penalty provided by this article, any violation of this article shall constitute a public nuisance and may be subject to restraint by injunction.

The City Manager, or the City Manager's designee, shall inform the Commission of any violations of this article by any person or entity within fourteen (14) days of such violation.

§ 23-16 Supplemental regulations.

This article is not intended to replace the Florida Endangered and Threatened Species Act or any other applicable federal, state, or local laws, rules, and regulations. Rather, this article is intended to supplement those laws, rules, and regulations to ensure the protection of the burrowing owl. SECTION 2. Severability. In the event that any portion or Section of this ordinance is determined to be invalid, illegal or unconstitutional by a court of competent jurisdiction, such decision shall in no manner affect the remaining portions or Sections of this ordinance which shall remain in full force and effect.

SECTION 3. Effective Date. This ordinance shall become effective immediately after its adoption by the Cape Coral City Council.

ADOPTED BY THE COUNCIL OF THE CITY OF CAPE CORAL AT ITS REGULAR SESSION THIS ___ DAY OF _____ , 2019.

REFERENCES

Allen, Tom. 2014. "Private conversations with the photographer ".

American Bird Conservancy. 2021. "Cats and Birds." Accessed May 15. https://abcbirds.org/program/cats-indoors/cats-and-birds/.

American Birding Association. 2021. "ABA Code of Birding Ethics". Accessed May 15.

https://www.aba.org/aba-code-of-birdingethics/.

Bear, Cindy. 2021. "Cape Coral Burrowing Owls."

Bernard, Eileen. 1983. Lies That Came True. 1 ed. Anna Pub.

Birch, Kim Photographs of Desperation Housing

Bird Anatomy. 2010. "Anatomy: Parts of a Feather." Birds Outside my Window. Accessed May 15. https://www.birdsoutsidemywindow.org/2010/07/02/anatomy- partsof-a-feather/.

Brady, Ryan. 2004. "Nest lining behavior, nest microclimate, and nest defense behavior of Burrowing Owls." MS, Boise State University

Cape Coral Florida. 2010. "City of cape coral: Burrowing Owl Viewing Etiquette." Accessed May 15. http://www.billmajoros.com/photoalbum/categories/new/florida 2010 /owlmap.pdf.

Creative Commons. 2021. "Attribution-Share Alike 3.0 Unported (CC BY-SA 3.0)." Accessed May 15. https://creativecommons.org/licenses/by-sa/3.0/.

Evolution Berkeley. 2021. "Understanding Evolution: The origin of birds." Accessed May 15. https://evolution.berkeley.edu/evolibrary/article/evograms_06.

Florida Backroads Travel. 2021. "Florida Regional History." Accessed May 15. https:// www.florida-backroads-travel.com/floridaregional-history.html.

Florida Department of State. 2021. "Prehistoric Native People." Accessed May 15. https:// www.dos.myflorida.com/floridafacts/florida-history/prehistoric-native-people/.

Florida Historical Society. 2016. "Florida Frontiers "The Geologic History of Florida"." Accessed May 15. https://myfloridahistory.org/frontiers/article/141.

Florida Wildlife Conservation Commission. 2011. "Economic Benefits of Wildlife Viewing in Florida." Accessed May 15. https://myfwc.com/media/5067/2011-economics-benefits.pdf.

Grunwald, Michael. 2017. "The Boomtown That Shouldn't Exist." Cape Coral, Florida, was built on total lies. One big storm could wipe it off the map. Oh, and it's also the fastest-growing city in the United States. Politico Magazine. Accessed May 15. https://www.politico.com/magazine/story/2017/10/20/fastest-growing-city- america-florida-cape-coral-215724.

Holmes, Jack. 2020. Owl Photo with Anole. Photography Baton Rouge Louisiana

Howard, Alex. 2021. "City of Cape Coral fights to keep water levels stable as dry season approaches." NBC 2. https://nbc-2.com/news/environment/2021/02/24/ city-of-cape-coral-fights-to-keep-water-levels-stable-as-dry-season-approaches/.

Johnson, David. 2019. "Cape Coral Friends of Wildlife Burrowing Owl Festival."

Low Country Raptors. 2021. "Digger our Burrowing Owl ". Accessed May 15. https:// www.lowcountryraptors.org/burrowingowl.html.

National Audubon Society. 2014. "314 North American Bird Species

Threatened by Global Warming, Audubon Scientists Reveal in New Study." Accessed May 15. https://www.audubon.org/news/314-north-american-bird-species-threatened-global-warming-audubon-scientists.

Ogden, Lesley Evans. 2017. "The Silent Flight of Owls, Explained." Even large owls, like Barred and Barn Owls, manage to fly silently through the trees. How do they pull it off—and why? Audubon. Accessed May 15. https://www.audubon.org/ news/the-silent-flight-of-owls-explained.

Ortiz, Omar Rodríguez. 2020. "Marco Island pays homeowners $250 for 'starter' owl burrows as nesting season begins." Accessed May 15. https://eu.marconews.com/ story/news/2021/01/26/marco-islandpays-homeowners-250-successful-starter-owl-burrows/4221013001/.

Saskatchewan Burrowing Owl Interpretive Center. 2021. "Burrowing Owl Facts." Accessed May 15. https://www.skburrowingowl.ca/owlfacts/#toggle-id-3.

Stroud, Hubert B, and Mary K Kilmer. 2018. "Preserving Habitat for Athene cunicularia floridana (Florida Burrowing Owl): Challenges and Solutions from Cape Coral, Florida, USA."

The Cornell Lab. 2021. "All about birds." Burrowing Owl Life History. Accessed May

15. https://www.allaboutbirds.org/guide/Burrowing_Owl/lifehistory#.

Wikipedia. 2021a. "Nictitating membrane." Accessed May 15. https://en.wikipedia. org/wiki/Nictitating_membrane.

Wikipedia. 2021b. "Ogygoptynx." Accessed May 15. https://en.wikipedia.org/wiki/ Ogygoptynx.

Wikipedia. 2021c. "Ornimegalonyx." Accessed May 15. https://en.wikipedia.org/ wiki/Ornimegalonyx.

Zeiss, Betsy. 1983. The other side of the river: Historical Cape Coral. 1 ed.: B. Zeiss.

AUTHOR BIOGRAPHY

After moving to Cape Coral over 20 years ago, Beverly encountered her first Burrowing Owl and was hooked. She is a founding member of Cape Coral Friends of Wildlife. Beverly is a frequent speaker about the Burrowing Owls at local schools, colleges, Audubon organizations, and service organizations like Kiwanis, Lions, and Rotary International. She has appeared on the Wink TV morning show, the FGCU radio program, and a NatGeoWild TV program.

Beverly is also a tour guide for both the Annual Burrowing Owl Festival and the city-run Nature of Cape Coral bus tour.

Beverly is a retired Registered Nurse and lives in Cape Coral with her husband Lloyd, and two Bichon dogs and spends a lot of time looking out her front window at the Burrowing Owls living on her front lawn.

***In 2022, Hurricane Ian flooded much of the southern end of Cape Coral. The author's home was flooded, so all the furniture, cabinets, and appliances were ruined, and the drywall needed to be removed from the walls. Homes all over Cape Coral had massive piles of debris generated, so huge trucks with claws removed the debris. During the removal, the claws from the truck accidentally dug up the burrow on her front lawn. Thankfully, the owls were not there at the time, so they were not injured, but with the burrow gone, the owls are gone. A starter burrow will be installed to encourage the owls to return once the city returns to some normalcy.

Made in the USA
Columbia, SC
10 February 2024